Mediterranean Diet:

This Book Inlcudes: Mediterranean Diet for Beginners & Meal Prep for Beginners. How to Lose Weight in Simple and Healthy Way. Weight loss, Meal Prep & Fat Burn

MEDITERRANEAN DIET FOR BEGINNERS:

The Ultimate Mediterranean Cookbook with Amazing Recipes to Help Improve Your Health and Discover True Mediterranean Cuisine

Copyright 2018 by Andrea Gianakouli All rights reserved.

The follow eBook is reproduced below with the goal of providing information that is as accurate and reliable as possible. Regardless, purchasing this eBook can be seen as consent to the fact that both the publisher and the author of this book are in no way experts on the topics discussed within and that any recommendations or suggestions that are made herein are for entertainment purposes only. Professionals should be consulted as needed prior to undertaking any of the action endorsed herein.

This declaration is deemed fair and valid by both the American Bar Association and the Committee of Publishers Association and is legally binding throughout the United States.

Furthermore, the transmission, duplication or reproduction of any of the following work including specific information will be considered an illegal act irrespective of if it is done electronically or in print. This extends to creating a secondary or tertiary copy of the work or a recorded copy and is only allowed with express written consent from the Publisher. All additional right reserved.

The information in the following pages is broadly considered to be a truthful and accurate account of facts, and as such any inattention, use or misuse of the information in question by the reader will render any resulting actions solely under their purview. There are no scenarios in which the publisher or the original author of this work can be in any fashion deemed liable for any hardship or damages that may befall them after undertaking information described herein.

Additionally, the information in the following pages is intended only for informational purposes and should thus be thought of as universal. As befitting its nature, it is presented without assurance regarding its prolonged validity or interim quality. Trademarks that are mentioned are done without written consent and can in no way be considered an endorsement from the trademark holder.

Disclaimer

All content in this book including images, text, and all other formats are provided for informational purposes only. It is not intended, in any way, to be a substitute for the professional medical diagnosis, treatment, or advice. You should always seek medical advice from a healthcare professional with any question you may have regarding a medical condition.

Table of Contents

Introduction..8

Chapter 1 What is The Mediterranean Diet?............................9

Chapter 2 History of the Mediterranean Diet

Chapter 3 Mediterranean Diet: Colors, Taste & Health

Chapter 4 Popular Foods Of The Mediterranean Diet

Chapter 5 Benefits Of The Mediterranean Diet

Chapter 6 Meal Plans For A Week

Conclusion

Description

The Mediterranean diet has been studied by scientists for many years. All the findings show it is the healthiest diet and best lifestyle anywhere in the world. This is because it focuses on eating natural produce, healthy oils, fish and other products that are actually great for you.

It is easy to follow this diet if you view it as a lifestyle and not a diet. All the meals included in this diet are not only healthy and great for you but also very tasty. This is because there are lots of spices and herbs that are used to add flavor and make the food delicious.

Combining the Mediterranean diet with regular exercise and family time is the best approach. You will start living your best life ever with lots of great food, delicious fish, an occasional glass of wine and so much more. You will be healthy with lower risks of illnesses as well as a better outlook on life.

Introduction

Congratulations on downloading this book and thank you for doing so.

The following chapters will discuss the Mediterranean diet in great detail. This book will show you how to follow the Mediterranean lifestyle for ultimate health and wellbeing.

The Mediterranean diet has been touted as the healthiest lifestyle in the world. This is because it offers clean eating with a focus on natural products. Eating natural, healthy foods everyday will not just boost your health but will enable your body to fight infections, keep chronic conditions at bay, and increase longevity.

You will learn which foods you need to eat if you want to lose weight, which foods are excellent for keeping infections at bay and how to combat inflammation. Eating naturally comes easy, and the Mediterranean diet makes it even easier with its delicious and tasty meals.

There are plenty of books on this subject on the market, thanks again for choosing this one! Every effort was made to ensure it is full of as much useful information as possible, please enjoy!

Chapter1: What is the Mediterranean Diet?

The Mediterranean diet is a diet that is based on the traditional foods that communities in countries along the Mediterranean used to eat in the 1930s to 1960s. These countries include Spain, Italy, and Greece.

According to researchers, communities living along the Mediterranean have exceptionally low risk regarding lifestyle diseases compared to Americans. Numerous studies have been conducted and they all show that the Mediterranean diet is beneficial to our health and wellbeing. Observing this diet regularly will help prevent conditions such as strokes, heart attacks, type II diabetes, as well as premature death.

The World's Healthiest Diet

There are those that have claimed that the Mediterranean diet is one of the healthiest diets in the world. This is mainly because of the kinds of foods involved. This diet includes whole grains, vegetables, fruits, olive oil, legumes, and proteins like seafood and fish. Red meat is rarely consumed and perhaps only once a week or even a fortnight.

This diet focuses on foods and normal recipes of the Mediterranean style of cooking. While the Mediterranean diet is not your typical, run-of-the-mill diet, it is actually a lifestyle. You can think of it as a different way of eating and living. Following this lifestyle, you are able to make well-balanced food choices that boost your health and taste great while promoting weight loss and development of lean muscle.

Major Components of the Mediterranean Diet

If you wish to follow the Mediterranean diet lifestyle, then you need to understand its key components. These include the following;

- Eating mostly plant-based foods such as green leafy vegetables, fruits, and whole grains.
- Replacing butter and margarine with healthy oils like olive oil.
- Making use of spices and herbs for flavoring rather than salt.
- Eating moderate portions of poultry and eggs once a week or every two days.

- Limiting your intake of red meats to either weekends or a couple of times per month. You can also limit red meat consumption to three-ounce portions.
- Eating fish or fish products at least two times weekly.
- Having moderate sizes of yogurt and cheese daily, every other day or weekly.
- Drinking a lot of water each day.
- Drink some red wine but in moderation.

Even as you follow this healthy diet, you should avoid the unhealthy foods and ingredients indicated below. To be on the safe side, make sure that you read the labels carefully to identify and avoid these unhealthy foods.

- **Refined grains**: These include pasta made from refined grains and white bread.
- **Refined oils**: These include soybean oil, cottonseed oil, and canola oil.
- **Added sugars:** For instance, avoid ice cream, candies, soda, and table sugar.
- **Trans fats:** Make sure you find substitutes for butter and margarine.
- **Processed meats:** They include ham, sausages, hot dogs, and so on.
- **Highly processed foods:** Foods you buy at the grocery store as well as any items labeled **"diet"** or **"low fat"** and those that are processed at a factory.

Research into Mediterranean Diet

There is a lot of research that has been carried out on this diet. Most of the research examined the benefits and health implications. According to findings, following the Mediterranean diet lifestyle has been found to be very beneficial to human health. Researchers found that this diet helps to reduce levels of inflammation in the body. Inflammation is a risk factor for conditions such as stroke, heart attack, and Alzheimer's.

Other notable attributes of this lifestyle include better blood sugar regulation, improved weight loss, and reduced cancer risk, lower chances of depression and many others. All these claims have been closely examined and proven to be correct.

Numerous Diet Plans Out There

There are numerous diets plans out there. Many of these are restrictive. They put a limit on what you can eat or drink and what you cannot. The problem with these diets is not just the restrictions but also the temporary nature of outcomes. If you wish to lose weight, a diet plan can help you lose weight which you regain once you are done with it.

The good news is that the Mediterranean diet is not simply a diet but a lifestyle. If you choose this diet as a lifestyle, then you can expect to lose weight and keep it off. You will also enjoy all the other benefits of this lifestyle. The Mediterranean diet will not require that you drop everything that you love and appreciate about food. Rather, you are permitted to make simple changes to your diet over time to make it a lifestyle and not a challenge.

Fortunately, the Mediterranean diet is different. It is a lifestyle and diet that mimics the life and eating habits of people living in places like Southern Italy and Greece in the 1940s, 1950s, and 1960s.

Rather than go on a diet for a fixed period of time, you will mostly endeavor to eat meals or dishes that are high in the foods already discussed above. These include unrefined cereals, moderate consumption of dairy products, low consumption of red meat and other non-fish meat products.

Evidence-Based Benefits

There is evidence available that this diet actually lowers your risk of heart and cardiovascular disease and even death. It is believed that olive oil is the major ingredient that promotes health in this diet.

This diet has become so significant that the United Nations, through its cultural branch, UNESCO, has identified this diet as an inherent part of the culture of countries across the Mediterranean including Croatia, Cyprus, Greece, Portugal, Morocco, and Spain.

The United Nations chose this diet because it involves a lot of symbols, knowledge, traditions, rituals, and skills concerning food processing, cooking, fishing, animal husbandry, crops harvesting and even the sharing and consumption of food.

About the Mediterranean Diet

This diet offers you a cuisine that is rich in flavors, colors, aromas, taste, and memories. The diet also supports the spirit and taste of all those who are in harmony with nature.

Not many people know how to correctly follow this diet and the associated lifestyle. While many talks about the Mediterranean diet, only a few follows it properly. This tends to generate a lot of confusion. Some think it constitutes a pizza with some meat or seafood, others think it is all about noodles and meat.

However, the Mediterranean diet is simple yet very healthy. A good diet aims to combine and balance food such that it satisfies the quantitative and qualitative needs of a person. In essence, a good diet is more of a lifestyle thana way of eating. It helps to preserve good health by making use of nutrients that enable the body to perform optimally all its vital functions.

This diet shows that it is possible to combine the goodness and taste of a meal ensuring it also provides health benefits. Consumers can be guaranteed of a dish that is delicious and tasty, yet still healthy and nutritious. Studies have consistently proven that Mediterranean cuisines make use of a wide variety of tasty food choices that include strong scents and inviting colors that are all in line with excellent health.

Chapter 2: History of the Mediterranean Diet

Historical Origins of the Mediterranean Diet

The Mediterranean basin covers more than 22 countries in Europe, Africa, and Asia. The diet of the communities living around this basin consists abundantly of plant foods like whole grains, legumes, seeds and nuts, olive oil, and fresh fruits and vegetables. There are only a few regional differences of this diet, and these differences are of little consequence to the diet because of numerous similarities. The origins of this diet reflect on the intricate interactions of civilizations and diverse populations over centuries.

Traditional Mediterranean Diet

The diet of the people living in the countries surrounding the Mediterranean Sea, such as Morocco, Spain, Greece, Italy and France were thought to be a poor man's diet. This traditional diet largely developed over thousands of years. The inhabitants of these lands labored to produce food and sustenance very poor terrain.

Some of the plants that grew here include grapevines, olive trees, and capers/ capers have an intense flavor. The olive tree is a symbolic plant that symbolizes all the plants growing in the region. It is also significant to the three largest religions of the Mediterranean. These are Christianity, Islam, and Judaism.

The local dishes of the Mediterranean were largely influenced by a rich history of different ethnic cultures from Italian to Spanish to Arabian. This region has for centuries been a center for culture and a crossroad for civilizations. As early as 3000 B.C., the region was occupied by Carthaginians, Romans, and Phoenicians among others.

Traditional Dishes over the Years

Traditional meals back then were heavily influenced by culture and foods available. Most of the dishes consisted of seafood, potatoes, eggplant, and tomatoes. The foods were flavored with spices originating mostly from North Africa. Families simply looked at their gardens to determine what to eat for dinner. The dishes then were very simple. They consisted mainly of local ingredients because importing food back then was very expensive. Sugar, for instance, was expensive to import, so they used honey and natural sweeteners instead.

While there was plenty of fish and seafood in their diets, residents of the Mediterranean coast were more of farmers than fishermen. Even then, iconic dishes such as pesto were common. They were made of garlic, raw tomatoes, olive oil and basil. Another iconic dish is fish couscous. It consists of a wide variety of vegetables, local seafoods, and legumes. Pantescan salad is a salad that was made with red onions, tomatoes, potatoes, and capers.

Caponata was a popular dish that consists of capers, eggplant, and olive oil. All these local dishes were common across the Mediterranean with small variations here and there. All these local foods are full of flavor, rich, and hearty. They are flavored with wild herbs, olive oil, and capers.

Public Acknowledgement of Mediterranean Diet

The Mediterranean diet was first publicly acknowledged by Ancel Keys, an American biologist, and his wife, Margaret Keys, a chemist in 1960s. However, it did not quite gain publicity or widespread recognition until the early 1990s. Studies from cities such as Madrid in Spain and Naples in Italy were the first sources of information on the usefulness and benefits of this diet.

Studies were conducted across the seven main countries of the Mediterranean and published in the 1970s. A report released in the 1980s closely followed the studies. Walter Willett of Harvard University's School of Public Health is credited as being the first person to produce a widely accepted version of the Mediterranean Diet. His publication was released in the mid-1990s.

High Amounts of Fat Consumed

Researchers participating in this study were amazed by the high amounts of fat the residents of Mediterranean countries consume. This is why most people at the time thought it was a paradox. The paradox is that these people tend to consume high amounts of fat but have some of the lowest rates of heart and cardiovascular diseases compared to people living in America.

Back then, people were amazed at this paradox mostly because of the high amounts of fat consumed but almost no signs of heart disease. In countries far from the Mediterranean such as England, residents consumed high levels of fats but were not as healthy. This is what was referred to as the French Paradox.

The French Paradox

The French Paradox is simply a catchphrase that was first used in the 1980s. This phrase refers to the apparent paradox based on observation. French citizens were found to have low levels of heart and cardiovascular conditions despite consuming a diet that is rich in saturated fats.

This was in great contrast to the general acceptance at the time that regular consumption of foods rich in saturated fats is a high-risk factor for coronary heart disease and other cardiovascular diseases. The paradox in this instance is that if the science linking saturated fats to coronary heart disease is true, then the French ought to have significantly high instances of heart diseases compared to countries where diets consist of low amounts of saturated fats.

Two possibilities are implied in the French Paradox. One possibility is that there exists a link between coronary heart disease and saturated fats, but the French lifestyle or diet mitigates against the risk. If this factor is identified, then it could explain the paradox. The other possibility is that no valid hypothesis links saturated fats to coronary heart disease.

The presumption with this paradox is that if the factor that mitigates the risk is identified, and then it can be applied to diets and lifestyles in other countries. This could help save lives so that people are healthier just like the French.

The French Diet

It has been observed over the years that the French diet lacks Trans fats is quite rich in short-chain saturated fatty acids. A researcher known as Frank Cooper noted in his book, "**Cholesterol and the French Paradox**," that the French Paradox is really because there are no Tran's fats and hydrogenated fats in the French diet.

There is a huge difference between the French and American diets. The American diet consists largely of huge amounts of hydrogenated vegetable oils while the French diet consists of natural saturated fats such as that found in cheese, nuts, and cream. These are easy for the human body to metabolize. The hydrogenated fats common in the American diet are difficult to metabolize and are associated with certain health risks.

Comparing the French Diet to the Mediterranean Diet

- People of the Mediterranean get almost 80% of their fats directly from vegetable and dairy sources such as cheese, whole milk, and whole milk yogurt. This shows the diet consists mostly of good fats. Americans, on the other hand, consume mostly unhealthy hydrogenated fats.
- Mediterranean people consume much higher quantities of fish compared to Americans. Fish contain healthy oils that contain omega 2 fatty acids.
- They eat smaller portions and divide their meals into courses. This allows food already consumed to be digested before more food is added.
- They also prefer products with full fat but without added sugar. They generally have a lower sugar intake. Americans consume large amounts of sugar directly and indirectly. Most no-fat and low-fat foods usually contain large amounts of sugar.
- The Mediterranean residents consume fewer snacks between meals. They also tend to avoid unhealthy options like carbonated drinks, snacks, deep fried foods, and most processed foods.
- They eat three meals per day but without snacking at all.
- They consume sufficient amounts of water, soups, and herbal tea.
- They prefer small quantities of high-quality food compared to Americans who sometimes prefer large amounts of low-quality foods.

- The Mediterranean people always seat down to eat their meals and savor each mouthful.
- They focus more on balance, freshness, variety, and pleasure.

Aspects of the Mediterranean Diet

1. Whole Diet – Scientists have noted that it is not a single nutrient that makes the Mediterranean diet so beneficial but rather a combination of nutrients that are inherent in unprocessed foods such as fruits, vegetables, nuts, and so on. In fact, the Mediterranean diet did not really focus on the amount of protein or fats consumed but the entire content of nutrients in a meal as sourced from natural foods. The focus was never on processed foods but only natural foods.

2. Greater Vegetable and Fruit - It has now become evident that a higher intake of vegetables and fruits in a diet will significantly reduce the risk of cardiovascular diseases.

3. Early Life Nutrition – Another reason why the Mediterranean diet is thought to be superior to the American diet is largely due to the dietary improvements within a child's early years of life. Dietary improvements are extended to kids throughout the generations.

Some governments made a deliberate effort to introduce aggressive nutrition programs that provide excellent nutrition and quality foods to young children and pregnant women to have a healthy population. This great nutrition goes on to explain the low levels of heart disease and obesity across countries bordering the Mediterranean.

The Mediterranean Diet in Portugal

Researchers studying this diet compared it to the American diet and diets of developed countries. During the study, some researchers referred to the Mediterranean diet as the diet of the poor. The researchers also thought that Portugal had the purest form of the Mediterranean diet. The problem is that, back then in the 1960s and 1970s, the dictator of Portugal did not want his country associated with the diet of the poor.

The Portuguese preferred to refer to their diet as the "**Atlantic Diet**." This diet is really the Mediterranean diet but with lots more seafood, fish, and green leafy vegetables.

Chapter 3: Mediterranean Diet: Colors, Taste, & Health

The Mediterranean diet has its origins in the Mediterranean basin. Some scientists consider this region to be the cradle of society. This is because the history of the ancient world actually took place here. More advanced civilizations such as the Egyptians existed across the Mediterranean along the banks of the Nile River.

According to the United Nation's cultural body UNESCO, the Mediterranean diet is defined as a lifestyle, a way of life, and a social practice. It involves knowledge and traditions ranging from fishing, cultures, conservation, harvesting, processing, fishing, preparation, and cooking food in a particular way.

Mediterranean Food Model

The Mediterranean diet is also known primarily as a food model. It enhances the safety and quality of food as well as links to the land. The meals offer a basic cuisine that is rich in taste, flavors, and nutrition. It takes total advantage of all the aspects of what is considered to be a healthy diet. This diet is ideally an ethical choice that maintains the customs and traditions of the inhabitants of the Mediterranean basin.

Consuming this diet on a regular basis is absolutely nourishing. It does have a profound effect on the health of an individual. The good nutrition involved helps to prevent metabolic diseases like hypertension, diabetes, and obesity. The Mediterranean diet does affect the health of families and communities because quality nutrition helps to maintain excellent health level and prevent diseases. Experts are of the opinion this diet is a useful resource that enables sustainable development which is superbly useful to the nations living around the Mediterranean and all over the world and also the cultural and economic effect of food.

Colors, Flavors, and Health at Center of the Mediterranean Diet

A lot of the health benefits associated with the Mediterranean diet can be attributed to Ancel Keys, an American research scientist from the University of Minnesota. She is the expert who was able to identify the correlation between this diet and cardiovascular diseases. Her research was as a result of intrigues because the relatively poor residents of the Mediterranean region were a lot healthier than their much wealthier counterparts in major cities like New York and London.

Keys pondered about this for a while and decided that it had something to do with the food and this is the reason why he led an expedition to learn more about the Mediterranean diet. Results for the study concluded that the diet actually presented a very low cholesterol rate in the blood. Because of this, people suffered less from the heart and coronary conditions. The main reason for this was the regular use of products such as pasta, olive oil, vegetables, bread, garlic, herbs, and red onions among numerous others. Also, most of the products used were of vegetable origin with very little use of red meat.

This was not the only study conducted by American scientists. It is safe to state that numerous other studies were conducted on the health benefits of the Mediterranean diet. There were points of convergence derived from these studies. One of these was the total recognition of the numerous beneficial qualities of this way of eating and living. Numerous studies as well clinical studies have repeatedly shown the many benefits and advantages of the Mediterranean diet. This is why it is viewed more as a lifestyle than a diet by many.

Of notable benefit is the diet's ability to reduce abdominal circumference, increase good cholesterol or HDL, reduce the presence of dangerous fats or triglycerides, reduces blood sugar levels, and also lowers blood pressure. It is important to note that the diet on its own will not be able to produce these amazing results. It is important to note that these benefits are not automatic, and people have to take deliberate steps to enjoy these benefits. Some risk factors have to be modified.

Some of the important factors that need to be modified include regular physical activity, quitting smoking, intake of sufficient but not excess calories and so on. It is also important to control any metabolic diseases such as obesity, diabetes, and hypertension. Leading a stress-free life or at least managing stress appropriately is definitely advisable. Eating a balanced diet and generally leading a disciplined lifestyle is absolutely recommended.

Middle Ages

Ancient Roman traditions greatly influenced the diet of the communities living along the Mediterranean coast. Some of the foods associated with Roman and Greek influence include wine, bread, and oil products. These were also seen as the symbols of the rural culture back then. This food options back then also included sheep cheese, seafood, fish, a variety of vegetables like lettuce, mallow, mushrooms, chicory, and leeks, and a little bit of red meat.

Not far from here, in the Germanic regions, pig fat was used for cooking and the little grain produced was not used for food but fermented to produce beer. These were introduced into the Mediterranean region but were not assimilated by the population. However, across the Mediterranean were the Arab lands of Morocco and others. The Arab and Muslim regions had developed their own food culture which was rather unique.

A lot of the foods within the Mediterranean diet are derived from the Islamic influence of the Mediterranean region. Muslims introduced agriculture to the region and derived a lot of their food from it. Some of the food crops they cultivated include eggplant, rice, citrus, sugar cane, spices, and spinach. Their cuisines consisted of other products from Europe such as almonds, lemons, orange, rose water, and pomegranates.

It is clear, therefore, to observe how foods from European hinterland were unable to influence the Mediterranean diet but Muslim and North African food cultures did. Later on, other foodstuffs were introduced into the Mediterranean diet. This happened when the Europeans "**discovered**" America. This opened a whole new world of exotic foods. Some of the foods that were introduced from the New World include tomatoes, potatoes, chili, pepper, tomatoes, a wide variety of beans among others.

Vegetable versus Cereal

The tomato was considered an ornamental fruit initially and later became the first red vegetable before eventually becoming the symbol of the Mediterranean cuisine. While the tomato is considered one of the most crucial vegetables of this diet, then the role played by cereals cannot be overlooked.

Cereals provide the basis of simple cooking as well as a tool for day-to-day survival. Cereals helped to fill the stomachs of hungry masses and were viewed as a weapon of survival especially for the poor people. There are different types of cereals, and these are prepared differently and consumed for different purposes. Among other things, they were used to prepare soups, bread, couscous, pasta, polenta, and paella.

The similarities between the diets or foods consumed by the residents of the Mediterranean have definitely been influenced by foods from the new lands of Americans, the Muslim communities, and foods our ancestors consumed.

Nutritious Diet

The Mediterranean diet is a nutritious diet that has universal acceptance and appreciation. Consuming this diet supports all aspects of our health. It is a fact that feeding or eating has a profound effect on the health of the individual. This is basically because good nutrition helps to manage acceptable levels of health as well as prevent non-contagious diseases like hypertension or high blood pressure, cancer, diabetes, and coronary heart conditions.

American nutritionists describe the Mediterranean diet as homemade minestrone and pasta dishes of wide varieties with a sprinkling of parmesan, tomato sauce, macaroni, small fish and few pieces of meat, and freshly baked bread still hot from the oven. This diet also includes fresh fruit for dessert and lots of vegetables sprinkled with olive oil.

Diet Rich in Fiber

It is safe to conclude that the Mediterranean diet contains a wide variety of nutrients and is rich in antioxidants, fiber, and unsaturated fats. This way, it helps reduce our consumption of cholesterol and animal fats.

The Food Pyramid

There are some concepts about the Food Pyramid. One of these is proportionality. This simply means we should choose the right amount of food from each food group. The other is portion which stands for the standard quantity of food that is to be consumed.

We also have variety, and it simply implies the opportunity to choose foods from. At the bottom of the Mediterranean diet food, pyramid are grains. There is a wide variety of grains to choose from. They constitute pasta, bread, rice, grains, and potatoes. Grains are followed up the pyramid by fruits of all kinds. Fruits are vegetables are therefore an important aspect and are ranked as such. There is a wide variety to choose from so that a different variety is consumed each day.

After the fruits and vegetables on the food pyramid are the legumes, olive oil, yogurt, and low-fat cheese. These should be consumed on a daily basis without fail. While meat is included, it does not rank highly. There is a preference of poultry such as chicken and turkey or even rabbit instead of beef. Beef is basically consumed rarely, perhaps only once or twice per month.

The pyramid showcases interchangeability. This essentially implies that you have a wide variety of foods to choose from within each group. Variety is crucial for sustaining this lifestyle.

In conclusion,therefore, we can deduce that the Mediterranean diet provides a great culture for the people of the Mediterranean region and beyond especially through food. It offers an immense source of tasty, delicious recipes and foods. The people of the Mediterranean and the communities living in this region consume foods that they generally produce within their region.

It has been established by nutritionists and health scientists that eating this diet on a regular basis is bound to provide the body with all the nutrients it needs. The diet can prevent numerous diseases, especially those of the metabolic type. This diet has been touted by medics as a source of excellent health for the body. It also promotes longevity among other benefits. It finds acceptance by both patients and medics across America and numerous places all over the world.

Chapter 4: Popular Foods of the Mediterranean Diet

The food groups of the Mediterranean diet have people thinking this could be the perfect solution for anyone thinking of embarking on a healthy journey and living a healthy and sustainable lifestyle.

We have already established by now that the Mediterranean diet is rich in vegetables and fruits, whole grains, nuts and seeds, olive oil, fish, and seafood. It is low in red meat and completely free of artificial sugars and refined foods.

A Lifestyle, Not just a Diet

The Mediterranean diet offers you a lifestyle and not just a diet. If you choose this lifestyle, then you will be consuming only wholesome foods with ingredients that are excellent for your body. You will not have to be counting carbs as is the case with other diets and will not necessarily be required to eat five meals each day.

Instead, you will have to eat real food and give up most, if not all, processed foods out there. There is evidence that proves this diet is great for you. The evidence shows that this diet actually improves your health and gives you a better quality of life. Other improvements that you will experience include long-term, permanent weight loss and reduced risk of chronic illnesses.

Flavors

Apart from the healthy foods, the Mediterranean diet also features amazing flavors that are rich and sumptuous. They make the food not only tasty but also very nourishing. This is the diet that brings together tasty food that is full of flavor yet healthy and nutritious.

It is no wonder that a lot of expert tout this diet, and lifestyle, as one of the best and healthiest in the entire world. Basically, if you wish to eat foods that are great for your health and beneficial for your well being, then the following food types are highly recommended.

Here is a closer look at foods that constitute the Mediterranean diet that you should eat regularly.
1. Almonds

Almonds are great for some reasons. First, they help you lose weight and keep it off. They also taste great as nut butter, as milk, and even as a snack. They are packed with healthy oils and lots of nutrients. While they are high in fats, almonds contain the good kind of fat that is excellent for the heart. They come highly recommended because they are highly nutritious and extremely healthy.

If you work out on a regular basis, then almonds can help you lose weight faster. They also help you feel full, so you do not have to eat a lot during meal times.

Almonds are a healthy snack that you can have in the morning, afternoon or evening. They are high in proteins and also healthy, heart-friendly fats. Other nutrients found in nuts include magnesium, manganese, vitamin E, healthy fats, and fiber. Almond nuts also contain phosphorus, vitamin B2, and trace elements like copper.

Just a handful of nuts will nourish your body and pump it full of excellent nutrients. You will also get plenty of antioxidants because almonds are a fantastic source of antioxidants.

Almonds are rich in Vitamin E which refers to a group of fat-soluble antioxidants. In fact, almonds are among the best source of vitamin E in the world. Studies have linked low levels of heart disease to this powerful vitamin.

2. Broccoli

Broccoli belongs to the cabbage family. It is a common Italian dark greenvegetable. It is rather bitter to the taste but packs in lots of nutrients and goodness including vitamin C, phytonutrients, carotenoids, potassium, and calcium among numerous others. This is why it is popularly referred to as a nutrition superstar and a "**super vegetable**." The fiber and carotenoids among other powerful nutrients help to keep dangerous conditions like cancer at bay. Fiber also promotes gut health and is directly linked to weight loss.

Other important and noteworthy nutrients found in broccoli include vitamin K, potassium, iron, and protein. However, what we may not be aware of is that broccoli is about 90% water with 3% protein and 7% carbs. It contains no fat and is very low in calories. One cup gives you only 31 calories, so you can consume it without worrying about weight gain.

The carbs found in broccoli are mostly sugars and fiber. The sugar is largely glucose and fructose with tiny amounts of maltose and lactose. Even then, the carbohydrate level is very low and measures about 3.5 grams per cup.

Trace elements and plant compounds found in broccoli include antioxidants, indole-3-carbinol, sulforaphane, carotenoids, and quercetin. These all assist the body fight diseases, combat inflammation, lower blood pressure, and contribute to eye health.

3. Wild Salmon

A lot of people may not be aware but swapping steak and ordering fish is actually an excellent idea. Not only is the fish absolutely delicious but is nutritious and good for your health. It is, however, advisable to choose wild salmon rather than farm-raised because the latter is usually soy fed and lack the immense benefits that wild salmons have. Research shows that salmon is one of the most nutritious foods in the world. It is loaded with nutrients and can reduce the risk factors of numerous diseases.

Salmon is delicious and popular among the residents of the Mediterranean. It is packed full of oils rich in omega-3 fatty acids. You get almost 2.5 grams in every 100 grams or 3.5 ounces of salmon. Omega-fatty acids are considered essential because they cannot be created by the body. Health experts recommend a daily intake of between 250 – 500 grams of omega-3 fatty acids that are rich in both DHA and EPA. This is equivalent to consuming 2 servings of salmon per week.

Farm raised salmons are packed rich in omega-6 fatty acids which are not good for your body. If you wish to get the best salmon, simply go down to the local fish market then ask for wild salmon. They have only 39 grams of protein per serving. Protein is an essential nutrient that should be obtained from your diet. It performs some crucial functions in the body.

4. Garlic

Garlic is largely considered a superfood because it is a powerful ingredient packed with numerous nutrients. Hippocrates, the father of modern medicine, used to prescribe garlic to treat various ailments. It is also widely used to add flavor to a wide variety of foods that are consumed in this diet. Garlic can be added to all sorts of foods including pasta and vegetables.

This little plant is capable of working with most foods well. Garlic is packed rich with vitamins such as vitamin B6 and nutrients such as manganese. It is powerful enough to rid the body of viruses, bacteria, and fungus of all kinds. A lot of these health benefits inherent in garlic have been confirmed by modern science.

Garlic's has numerous healing properties. It can combat the common cold, cure skin ailmentsregulate the heartbeat, and so much more. It also lowers your bad cholesterol levels and improves good cholesterol. This is why adding garlic to your meals is very important.

5. Chickpeas

Beans are full of goodness including nutrients such as white protein, starch, as well as calcium, folate, zinc, and iron. Chickpea is a popular legume that can be eaten regularly together with other foods. It is known by other names too such as garbanzo beans and Bengali gram. It is round and cream in color and is popular not just in Mediterranean countries but across Asia and Africa. It is sometimes combined with other grains, beans, and starches to provide a delicious yet healthy meal. It is not just healthy but also fills you up.

Chickpeas contain both insoluble and soluble fiber as well as phytosterols and phytates. Studies show that chickpea is able to assist the body fight off conditions such as diabetes, minimize heart disease risks and also prevents colon cancer. It is one of the initial grains domesticated by early man. Chickpeas were a staple food consumed regularly by ancient Egyptians, Romans, and Greeks.

Chickpeas are treasured across the Mediterranean because they are tasty and contain numerous minerals, trace elements, and other nutrients. They include healthy fats, carbohydrates, fiber, B-vitamins, potassium, calcium, molybdenum, iron, zinc, phosphorus, magnesium, and phosphorus.

6. Quinoa

One of the many ways of enjoying your quinoa is by preparing a delicious quinoa soup. Quinoa is also considered a superfood that is rich in numerous amounts of nutrients. Quinoa is naturally gluten-free and is a great source of protein. Just one cup of this amazing vegetable has about 5 grams of fiber and 8 grams of protein. It contains plenty of useful nutrients and minerals such as magnesium and calcium. Others are protein, fiber, manganese, phosphorus, folate, copper, iron, and zinc. It also contains trace minerals like phytic acid, oxalates, and quercetin.

While it has a mild flavor, it has a pleasant taste and tastes really great when cooked in foods like chicken stock or coconut milk. However, the bitter version has a lot more antioxidants compared to the sweet varieties. Even then, both serve as an excellent source for both minerals and antioxidants. In fact, quinoa has been found to have the highest antioxidant content of most cereals, legumes, and pulses.

Quinoa provides 16% protein per dry weight. It is considered by nutritionists as a complete protein source because it contains all the essential amino acids. These are important because they constitute the building blocks of all cells and tissue in our bodies. Quinoa contains a sufficient amount of fiber which is excellent for the digestive system. You get 10% fiber per dry weight of quinoa. Insoluble fiber is known for reducing your risk of diabetes while soluble fiber feeds bacteria in the gut to enhance and improve your digestive system.

7. Chia Seeds

Chia seeds are considered to be among the healthiest foods in the world. They come loaded with tons of nutrients that can do the body a lot of good. Chia seeds are the planet's greatest source of vitamin C and contain other useful nutrients including fiber, magnesium, protein, fat, manganese, calcium, vitamins, and so much more.

An ounce or 28 grams of chia seeds consists of 30% manganese, 18% calcium, 9 grams of fat that includes omega-3, 4 grams of proteins and 11 grams of fiber. Chia seeds also contain vitamin B3, Vitamin B1, potassium, zinc, and vitamin B2. This single ounce has only 137 calories with only 1 gram of carbohydrates. This is why chia seeds are considered extremely nutritious.

They will keep you satisfied and provide you with sufficient fiber for your system. There are numerous ways of consuming these seeds such as adding them to your yogurt or oatmeal and even a breakfast smoothie. Since they have almost no flavor, they will nicely blend with any food that you choose.

The benefits of chia seeds can be summarized to show that they deliver a massive amount of nutrients with very few calories. Never be deceived by the size of the seeds. While they may be tiny, they pack a powerful nutrition punch. Chia seeds are a whole grain food that is often grown organically, is free of gluten yet never genetically modified. This is why it is the world's best source for some nutrients.

8. Egg Plant

The eggplant is also known as the aubergine and is part of the nightshade family of plants. It is loved for its neutral flavor and rare texture. It is capable of blending well in sauces and introducing amazing flavors and aromas. While many consider it a vegetable, it is a fruit because it grows from a flowering plant and has seeds. There is a wide variety of eggplants with the most common being the variety with deep purple skin.

It provides meaty satisfaction to cuisines and is very popular in most Mediterranean dishes. While it does not contain as many nutrients as the superfood, it is beloved because of its effects on flavors. The eggplant is rich in nutrients that include minerals, vitamins, and trace elements.

It contains potassium and fiber as well as phytonutrients and chlorogenic acid that give it cancer-fighting and antiviral properties. It also contains protein, vitamin K, vitamin C, folate, magnesium, manganese, and carbs. Trace elements available include copper and niacin. It is, therefore, rich nutrients that are great for your body and for great health.

Eggplant is high in antioxidants. These antioxidants help protect the body from different kinds of chronic illnesses like cancer and heart disease. Eggplants are quite rich in a type of pigment known as anthocyanin. These are powerful antioxidants that your body needs. It protects against cell damage.

9. Eggs

Eggs are normally referred to as nature's multivitamin basically because they are so nutritious. They can go be consumed with most meals and have a host of benefits for your body. This means the entire egg and not just the white portion. Scientists have shown that the yolk is really the best part of the egg. It contains choline which aids in weight loss. There are numerous ways of preparing eggs including preparing delicious omelets and even baking some muffins. Eggs contain plenty of protein as well as the good cholesterol. You can find out the numerous ways of preparing eggs so that they are delicious, full of flavor as well as nutrients.

Eggs contain powerful nutrients and unique antioxidants that are essential for the brain that most people lack. Just a single egg contains sufficient nutrients to nourish a fertilized egg. These nutrients include good fats, minerals, high-quality proteins, a range of vitamins and lots of trace minerals and other less-known nutrients. These nutrients found in eggs include vitamin A, vitamins B2, B12, B5, and selenium. Other nutrients include folate, vitamin E, iron, calcium, zinc, potassium, and manganese among numerous others.

10. Ezekiel Bread

Ezekiel bread is the healthiest bread that you will ever find. This bread is a type of sprouted ancient grain bread, baked from some legumes and whole grains that have started germinating. It contains no added sugar and is a much better option than white bread and even whole grain bread as these contain processed floors and added sugars. If you have to eat bread, then always choose Ezekiel bread. It is healthier and better for you. You can find different versions of this bread some of which are flavored. A single slice of this bread has about 3 grams of fiber, yet it contains only 80 calories.

One major difference between Ezekiel bread and other types of bread is that it contains no added sugar. It is also made from sprouted, organic whole grains. The sprouting grains significantly alter the composition of the grains. Also, regular bread uses either processed wheat or pulverized whole wheat. However, Ezekiel bread consists of various legumes and cereal grains. These grains are barley, wheat, spelt, and millet while the legumes are lentils and soybeans.

11. Couscous

The base of most Mediterranean diets is usually unrefined grains such as barley, bread, couscous, and pasta. When grains remain whole and unprocessed, their glycemic index remains low. This way, they are digested slowly in the body and go through the entire system slowly and methodically.

Couscous has for a long time been a delicacy of the people living in North Africa. However, it is now an integral part of the Mediterranean diet and is consumed in many other places around the world. There are generally three different types of couscous. These are the Moroccan, Lebanese, and Israeli. They all have the same amazing benefits especially in terms of nutrition.

Selenium

Selenium is known for its anticancer properties. It helps lower your risk of cancer and also battles precursors to cancer. Scientists conducted a study that showed high selenium levels in the body to improve the body's fight against cancer. Other studies show an increase in the risk of cancers like prostate due to lower levels of selenium.

Selenium also boosts your immune system so consuming couscous is good for protecting against infections and all other manner of attacks. Couscous is also a great source of plant protein. By consuming couscous on a regular basis, your body benefits from the protein it obtains. Not only do amino acids found in proteins contribute to building the body muscle but are important in most metabolic chemical reactions.

12. Hazelnuts

In Mediterranean countries such as Italy, olive trees and nut trees are very common. This means these important food products are readily available. Nuts are generally treasured as a delicious yet healthy snack. Hazelnuts are not just consumed as nuts but are sprinkled on salads and ground into sauces. They are mostly consumed raw or roasted and are sometimes ground into a paste.

Hazelnut is packed full of vitamins, fats, and minerals. The reason why hazelnuts are so valuable in the Mediterranean diet is that they contain monounsaturated fats. These monounsaturated fats are very good for the heart. Hazelnuts contain vitamin E, fiber, magnesium, calcium, and protein. Hazelnuts are high in calories. However, they contain important nutrients. Apart from these mentioned above, hazelnuts are also rich in carbs, thiamin, copper, manganese, and healthy fats. It also contains phosphorus, folate, zinc, and potassium. It is also a rich source of crucial mono and polyunsaturated fats that contain the all-important omega-6 and omega-9 fatty acids.

13. Olive Oil

Extra virgin olive oil is regarded as the best and healthiest oil in the world. There is always the controversy about oil, especially animal fats and seed oils. People worry about their effects on our bodies. When it comes to olive oil, however, there is no controversy and no question. Extra virgin olive oil is known to be healthy oil that is good for your body and especially good for your heart.

Olive oil is especially popular when it comes to preparation of vegetables. Extra virgin olive is cold pressed directly from olives and is extremely important for cooking and dressing salads.

The extra virgin variety is rich in antioxidants and monounsaturated fats. Scientists believe that olive oil is the primary reason why residents of Mediterranean have such few incidents of heart disease. It is also believed to help ward off cancer and reduce fat in the body, especially stubborn belly fat.

14. Greek Yogurt

What is Greek yogurt? This is strained yogurt that is different from your ordinary yogurt. The producers of this beverage add an extra step during the production process. This process eliminates excess lactose, water, and minerals. The remaining product is rich, creamy, yogurt that has a tart taste, less sugar, and plenty of carbs. Your body is able to absorb the nutrients easily because of the acidity.

Yogurt is very popular among Mediterranean residents, especially Greek yogurt and Skyr. Skyr is Icelandicyogurt. Greek yogurt is prepared using goat milk. Skyr yogurt is sieved repeatedly and uses additional milk to increase the texture and flavors. The yogurts from the region use only natural ingredients such as milk from grass-fed cows, fruit, and agave. It contains none of those artificial flavors, colors, and sugars. You can sprinkle some yogurt onto your chia seeds or add a chunk to your soup.

The best way to have this yogurt is in plain form with no flavors, coloring, or artificial additives. This yogurt has numerous health benefits, and it is advisable to make it part of your regular diet. Nutrients present in this particular yogurt include proteins, probiotics, calcium, and potassium among numerous others.

15. Chicken

Chicken is one of the most popular sources of white meat today. It is also among the world's most widely consumed meats. People love chicken because it is tasty and is an excellent source of white meat. White meat is a good source of protein if you are seeking to build lean muscle, lose fat, and maintain muscle mass.

Chicken also happens to be an excellent source of protein and can form part of your diet numerous times each week. Chicken can be seared, baked, or grilled. However, you should not deep fry it. You can eat chicken till you are full. This white meat is beneficial to your body as it contains lean protein which is desirable for muscle building. You can make an entire meal based out of chicken and vegetables or combine chick with other foods like rice and so on.

16. Variety of Peppers

Mediterranean cooking involves plenty of peppers. These are used in different formats including ground and dried, fresh and even roasted. They can be ground into a variety of pastes and sauces and used to add flavor and color to different Mediterranean dishes. In addition to flavor, they also come with numerous nutrients including vitamins C and A, folate, fiber, vitamin K, beta-carotene, and lots of others. They also contain lutein, lycopene, and zeaxanthin which offer protection against conditions such as macular degeneration.

17. Shrimp

Seafood is very popular among communities living along the Mediterranean coast. One of the staple seafood that is popular among these communities is shrimp. It is among the main sources of protein and quite nutritious. Seafood such as shellfish and fish are consumed a lot because of their relative availability. These contain the crucial omega-3 fatty acids.

However, specimens such as squid and shrimp add nutrients such as niacin, protein, and selenium to the diet. Shrimp is actually a type of shellfish. Other nutrients found in shrimp include iodine, vitamin B12, phosphorus, iron, magnesium, zinc, and phosphorus. It is actually one of the best sources of iodine and is rich in antioxidants as well.

18. Tomatoes

The tomato is a fruit of the plant from the nightshade family and is native to South America. People often mistakenly think that the tomato is a vegetable. It is still hard to believe that this delicious and powerful fruit is not native to the Mediterranean. Tomatoes are a staple in every Mediterranean dish today. You will hardly come across a dish without this ubiquitous orb.

Tomatoes come in different forms including paste, canned, and fresh. They are rich in nutrients such as lycopene, carotene, bio-flavanoids and vitamin C. Lycopene is a powerful antioxidant that protects you against cancer, especially prostate cancer. Tomatoes are versatile fruits that can be added to just about any cuisine.

19. Hummus

Hummus is popularly used as a spread for your bread and as a healthy dip. It is made by blending some healthy and quality products such as garlic, olive oil, tahini, chickpeas, lemon juice, and some choice spices. Hummus is a very tasty as well as nutritious spread. The chickpeas are able to curb hunger and are loaded with useful plant protein. You can use hummus with vegetables like cucumber and celery. Some of the more popular spices used to prepare this delicious spread include sun-dried tomato, roasted red pepper, black pepper, sage, or even spice jalapeno. While it is advisable to prepare your own at home, you can also buy hummus brands at the grocery store.

20. Cauliflower

Cauliflower is one of the most popular vegetables in the Mediterranean diet. It is an extremely healthy vegetable that can nourish the body and keep it in excellent health. It contains essential plant compounds that can reduce the risk of diseases like cancer and heart disease.

Cauliflower is used to prepare most dishes and is a useful ingredient because of the amazing flavor and great taste that it brings. It is also packed full of minerals and nutrients that are great for your health. It is great for weight loss and is easy to include in your regular diet.

Chapter 5: Benefits of the Mediterranean Diet

The Mediterranean diet has been touted as one of the world's best diets and lifestyles. The diet has been scientifically proven to be beneficial in numerous ways. This is mostly due to its emphasis on whole grains, high fiber intake, antioxidants, healthy fats, fish, fresh produce and moderate intake of red meat and alcohol.

By following this lifestyle, you will enjoy most meals with your family or loved ones as you can prepare most meals at home. Cooking together as a family and enjoying a glass of red wine afterward is the kind of lifestyle envisioned by the Mediterranean diet. This diet expects you to consume plenty of fresh produce that is non-starchy. You should aim for about 5 small meals throughout the day that include not just fresh produce but also some healthy oils. These oils can be from avocado, fish, nuts, or olive oil. Your meals should also include lots of fish, eggs, and dairy protein such as yogurt or cheese.

Health Benefits of the Mediterranean Diet

The Mediterranean diet is considered an ideal diet because you do not have to go to any extremes. You are able to enjoy a great quality of life and enjoy delicious, well-prepared foods that you and your loved ones will enjoy. You are allowed to eat regularly without skipping meals and so on. Once you begin living this lifestyle, you will shortly thereafter notice a lot of difference in your life. You should expect to notice a difference in your brain, heart health, and longevity.

1. The Mediterranean Diet Keeps You Agile with Age

The meals that you consume with your Mediterranean diet contain a lot of useful minerals, vitamins, essential oils, and numerous other nutrients. Because of all these nutrients, you should expect to benefit in various ways. For instance, you will have a lower risk of conditions such as fragility and muscle weakness.

Senior citizens who follow this diet have shown rapid improvement in their health with stronger bones and more muscle than their peers. Their risk for such conditions can be reduced by up to 70% by simply switching to this diet. If you want to lead this lifestyle successfully into your later years, begin by eating plenty of fresh vegetables, fruits, lean proteins and healthy fats. These will keep your muscles supple and lean, your bones strong and your body agile.

2. This Diet is Excellent for a Healthy Heart

Heart and coronary conditions are much lower across the Mediterranean than in the United States and other parts of the world. This can be directly attributed to diet choices of the communities living around the Mediterranean. According to experts, the healthy oils from nuts, salmon, and olives are great for the heart. They promote heart health and circulation.

Dietary choices also enhance good heart health. Remember that it is not just the food that you eat that matters but also what you drink. The Mediterranean diet also promotes an active lifestyle. It encourages physical activity as well as social support. A glass of wine taken occasionally and lots of healthy juices will support a healthy body and a healthy heart. Red wine has been linked to lower heart disease risks. However, you should limit your intake to about one or two glasses per day.

Moderation is a key to a healthy body. A good aspect to focus on is bad cholesterol. The Mediterranean diet promotes healthy oils that are great for the heart. It also helps to eliminate bad cholesterol that is often deposited in the arteries and causes cardiovascular problems.

3. It Protects against Type II Diabetes

Type II diabetes occurs when there is unregulated sugar in the blood. This often caused by excessive consumption of processed starch and high glycemic carbs. The Mediterranean diet has proven to be a lot more effective than all other diets in protecting against diabetes.

Scientists compared the Mediterranean diet against other diets that include vegan, vegetarian, high protein, high fiber, and numerous others. The results show that the Mediterranean diet is much more effective at combating diabetes compared to all others. Research scientists placed an emphasis on foods containing monounsaturated oils such as olive oil, fish such as salmon, vegetables, and fruits. These have been shown to lower cholesterol and blood sugar levels in people suffering from diabetes.

4. The Diet Reduces Chances of Developing Alzheimer's Disease

The Mediterranean diet includes foods that improve blood sugar, lower cholesterol and the overall health of your cardiovascular system. All these benefits work together and reduce your risks or chances of suffering from conditions like Alzheimer's.

There is research-based evidence that shows the Mediterranean diet helps protect against conditions like cognitive decline. This way, adults, especially seniors are able to limit the burden of illness and preserve or maintain their quality of life. Doctors advise patients to lead healthier lifestyles such as adopting the Mediterranean diet. Healthy eating habits, regular exercises, and keeping busy throughout the day all help in addressing conditions like dementia and similar cognitive conditions.

5. Lose Weight the Healthy Way

A lot of overweight and obese people struggle to lose weight. This is often because they do this the wrong way. Many opt for diets that are temporary or do not work. It is important to change lifestyle completely to enjoy the benefits inherent to the chosen lifestyle.

Losing weight through the Mediterranean diet comes in some ways. None of the recommended food items is actually fattening. All the carbs are low glycemic which means they are digested slowly and keep you feeling full longer. They do not contain any processed carbohydrates or starches or unhealthy oils.

To lose significant weight healthily, you should also lead an active lifestyle. For instance, you can engage in regular exercises on a regular basis. Alternatively, you can take deliberate steps to be active such as using the stairs often and walking to the grocery store. Finally, maintain your portions with every meal. You should not overeat because this is often the main cause of obesity.

6. Mediterranean Diet Helps Fight Cancer

Research scientists have proven that the Mediterranean diet can help fight against cancer. It has clearly demonstrated that a proper eating plan based on this diet can actually lead to reduced risk of cancer as well as cancer-related deaths. The foods that constitute the Mediterranean diet such as olive oil, eggs, salmon, and others contain numerous nutrients including trace elements, selenium, antioxidants, omega-3 fatty acids and many more.

All these nutrients work together to eliminate toxins in the body and remove waste from the cells. Antioxidants are effective in combating free radicals most of which are thought to be a prelude to cancer. Mediterranean diet plays a major role in the prevention of cancer. This lifestyle, in particular, helps to prevent the development of radical cancers such as postmenopausal breast cancer.

7. It Enhances Relaxation

When you adopt the Mediterranean lifestyle, you should also adopt other aspects to fully benefit from it. This means spending more time with your family, cooking and eating together and engaging in other families as well. By spending quality time with people that you have, you will relax your mind and enhance the release of the feel-good hormone.

These hormones such as serotonin calm you down and help you to relax. Calming your nerves and heart enhances overall health and promote longevity. Basically, eating nutritious meals and relaxing your mind and body gives you a more relaxed lifestyle.

8. The Mediterranean Diet Helps Fight Inflammation in the Body

Inflammation occurs within the body. When this happens, you are at risk of various major illnesses and your health will be compromised. The good news is that the Mediterranean diet helps reduce inflammation in the body. Studies have indicated a reduction in intensity of inflammation markers in high-risk individuals.

Inflammation is often caused by exposure to oxidative stress. The antioxidants contained in the Mediterranean diet are able to combat oxidative stress successfully. You can improve this action by eating more foods that contain choline such as soybeans and egg yolks as well as spinach and beetroots.

9. This Diet is Excellent for your Skin

The Mediterranean diet is excellent for your skin. The skin is a crucial organ that serves numerous purposes like protecting other organs and eliminating waste. If you consume plenty of vegetables and fruit, foods rich in antioxidants, olive oil and lots of water, then you will soon love the look of your skin.

Tomatoes protect the skin against free radicals and even against skin cancers due to sun exposure. Red wine in moderation is also a part of the Mediterranean diet. It contains antioxidants that are useful for the skin.

10. Mediterranean Diet Halves your Chances of Suffering Parkinson's Disease

Parkinson's disease is a debilitating disease that affects quality of life in later years. Fortunately, the Mediterranean diet provides you with sufficient amounts of antioxidants. The levels of antioxidants in this diet will help you cut your risks by half. These are found mostly in the healthy fats, seafood dishes, vegetables, and fruits that you eat.

The antioxidants protect your cells from exposure to oxidative stress. Oxidative stress damages cells and this can result in the development of debilitating diseases like Parkinson's.

11. It Protects Cognitive Health

The Mediterranean diet will help improve your cognitive ability. Scientists have proven that individuals who follow this diet have superior focus and attention as well as enhanced memory. The diet also enhances the brain's language capabilities. This is important for those who wish to maintain brain function throughout life as well as fending off dementia in elderly persons. You will experience a considerable enhanced quality of life even in your old age.

12. Mediterranean Diet Helps Improve Mood

This diet, and associated lifestyle, offers plenty of brain promoting benefits. People suffering mental health challenges such as ADHD, depression, and anxiety will definitely benefit from the Mediterranean diet.

The issues of anxiety and other mental health conditions usually occur due to dopamine deficiency. Dopamine is the enzyme responsible for mood regulation. Following this diet regularly will enable your body produce this chemical and keep your brain happy and mood elevated.

13. It Can Help with Pain Relief

Whole grains and fiber rich foods that are common in the Mediterranean region are rich in nutrients such as magnesium. Fresh fruits and green leafy vegetables can also contribute to your pain management plan. Such a diet can also help you reduce dependence on pain killers. Your body will respond to pain differently because the diet also combats inflammation and helps minimize stress levels. It is very possible that your chronic pain could disappear thanks to the Mediterranean diet.

Chapter 6: Meal Plans for A Week

The Mediterranean lifestyle requires that you eat specific types of foods. The diet is typically high in healthy plant food but low in animal foods. Even then, seafood and fish are highly recommended. Drink plenty of water, fruit and vegetable juices, and red wine. Tea and coffee are also allowed, but beverages with high levels of added sugars are not allowed.

This diet is basically focused on legumes, tubers, nuts and seeds, fruits, vegetables, whole grains, herbs and spices, poultry, dairy, eggs, and healthy fats. Experts believe that whole, single-ingredient foods are the key to excellent health.

Sample Menu for a Week

Here is a sample menu based on the Mediterranean lifestyle. Please keep in mind that nutritionists and health experts insist that there is no need to track macronutrients or count calories on the Mediterranean diet. You also don't need to eat more than three times per day, but snacking in-between meals is allowed.

Monday

- Breakfast: Oats with milk, Greek yogurt with strawberries
- Lunch: wholegrain chicken sandwich, tomatoes, onions and veggie salad

- Dinner: Tuna fish salad with olive oil and a succulent fruit

Tuesday

- Breakfast: Nuts and sliced fruits with yogurt
- Lunch: Mediterranean lasagna
- Dinner: Pan fried salmon served with vegetables and brown rice

Wednesday

- Breakfast: Tropical fruit and omelet with tomatoes, onions, and veggies
- Lunch: Wholegrain sandwich with fresh vegetables and cheese
- Dinner: Mediterranean lasagna left over from the previous day

Thursday

- Breakfast: raisins and oatmeal with fruits and nuts
- Lunch: leftover lasagna from the previous night
- Dinner: Vegetable salad with olives, tomatoes, and feta cheese

Friday

- Breakfast: veggies, omelet, and olives
- Lunch: wholegrain rice with cowpeas stew
- Dinner: roast potatoes, grilled chicken, vegetables, and fruit

Saturday

- Breakfast: vegetables and eggs pan fried with olive oil
- Lunch: Greek yogurt and strawberries, nuts and oats
- Dinner: Baked potato, a salad, and grilled lamb

Sunday

- Raisins and oatmeal with hazelnuts and a fruit
- Whole grain turkey sandwich with vegetables
- Lasagna with cheese, olives, and vegetables

Healthy Snacks to Accompany your Meals

Sometimes you may feel hungry during the day. Alternatively, you may wish to have a snack in the day or evening. You could always choose to have a snack. The Mediterranean lifestyle offers a wide variety of healthy snacks that are good for your health. Feel free to choose from one of these.

- Some grapes and berries
- Carrots
- A piece of fruit
- A handful of nuts or seeds
- Apple slices
- Greek yogurt

Simple Mediterranean Dishes you can Prepare at Home

1. Greek Fish Stew

This is a Greek cuisine that serves two to four people. It takes 5 minutes to prepare and about 30 minutes to cook.

Ingredients

- 1 ¼ cups of sliced and diced onions
- 4 cod fillets
- ¼ cup olive oil
- 1 cup of water
- 1 teaspoon of pepper
- 1 teaspoon of salt
- ¼ teaspoon each cayenne and paprika

Instructions

Add water to a pan and put it on the stove with medium heat. Then pour in the olive oil as well as the onions, cayenne, pepper, salt, and paprika. Let the mixture boil then reduce the heat. Allow it to simmer for a couple of minutes until the onions soften.

Now add the fish slices to the stew and let it continue simmering for about 5 to 10 minutes. Check to see if the fish is cooked and remove from the stove. If it is ready, serve on dishes with the onion mixture.

2. The Fattoush Salad

The Fattoush salad is a simple bread salad that is popular throughout North Africa and southern Europe. It consists of chopped salad dressed with line vinaigrette. It can be enjoyed with some pita chips. Ingredients do vary from one location to another, but the idea is the same.

Ingredients

- Cucumbers
- Tomatoes
- Lettuce leaves
- Green onions
- Radish
- Fresh herbs such as mint or parsley
- 2 loaves pita bread
- Salt and pepper
- Extra virgin olive oi

Preparation

Chop the vegetables and slice or dice the herbs to suit your needs. Make sure you always select the best produce at the grocery store. Prepare your own pita chips at home rather than buy at the store. Slice the pita bread and toast it to a crisp brown color.

Add the herbs to the chopped vegetables then pour in your extra virgin olive oils. If you can, always use the extra virgin olive oil. Other olive oils may not be pure simple because the extraction methods may have affected the purity and effectiveness. You can top up the dish with vinaigrette and even molasses if you like.

3. Chicory and Beans

This is a common dish across the Mediterranean. Inhabitants prefer eating their vegetables, pasta, and lentils during the week saving their meats for the weekends. The following dish serves 4 to 6 people and is of Italian background.

Ingredients

- 1 can of well rinsed and drained beans
- 2 to 3 medium heads of chicory
- 3 cloves of garlic
- 1 tablespoon of Olive oil
- ½ teaspoon of salt

Preparation

Soak your chicory in water then repeat this several times until it is clean then chop off the roots. Now boil the chicory in hot, salted water for about 10 minutes or until tender. Once it is tender, drain and reserves the water.

Take a large sauté pan and place on the stove with low heat. Pour in some olive oil and add the garlic. Let it brown then add red pepper. Remove the pan from the heat after a few minutes.

Now add the chicory to the seasoned oil and let the mixture simmer for 5 to 10 minutes. Add the boiled beans and the reserved (drained) water. Mix well and take care not to damage the beans.

4. Lemon Shrimp Pasta

This is a popular and delicious Italian dish that is easy to prepare and great for the whole family. Here is how to prepare the lemon shrimp pasta.

Ingredients

- 1 pound of shrimp
- 1 large red onion
- 4 cloves of garlic
- ½ cup of white wine
- 1 cup of chicken broth
- ½ tablespoon red hot chili pepper powder
- 1 lemon squeezed

Preparation

Take out the shrimp and thaw it out. Now slice the onion and dice the garlic then sauté them on a pan for just a couple of minutes. Toss in the shrimp and let it cook for a few minutes then pour in the white wine. Add the red-hot chili pepper and the lemon juice and allow it to cook for a few minutes.

Once it is cooked, let it simmer, so the shrimp is poached. Meanwhile, you could prepare the pasta at the same time. Once the pasta is boiled, you take it out and add to the skillet with the shrimp and sauce. You can add some chopped parsley and grated parmesan cheese.

5. Marinated Cod and Cabbage

Ingredients

- 6 cups of seafood broth
- ½ pound of codfish
- 1 dozen mussels
- 12 large shrimps
- 1 tablespoon sea salt
- 2 tablespoons of minced parsley
- 8 cloves of diced garlic
- 2 teaspoons of paprika
- 1 medium-sized, chopped onion
- 1 large, chopped tomato
- 1 diced red bell pepper
- Lemon wedges

Preparation

Prepare and heat the broth in a large pot. Add the fish and shrimp then sprinkle some salt and allow to simmer for 10 minutes. Mash some thyme, garlic, and parsley then add some salt and add to the mixture. Add water and pour in the paprika.

Put a pan on fire then add some olive oil. Once hot, add the shrimp and fish until brown. Add the bell pepper and onions then cook till the vegetables become soft. Now raise the heat and pour in the broth. Pour in the rice evenly and allow it to boil till ready or for three minutes. Now arrange the clams, shrimp, and mussels on top of the rice. Let the food sit on the heat for a couple of minutes so the rice cooks. You can then garnish the food with lemon wedges.

6. Chickpeas and Eggplant Salad

Ingredients

- 1 garlic clove skinned and bashed
- 1 large eggplant chopped up into cubes

- 1 can of well-drained chickpeas
- 1 teaspoon of paprika
- 4 tablespoons of extra virgin olive oil
- Pepper and sea salt for seasoning
- Parsley leaves

Preparation

Take a large sauté pan and heat the olive oil. Pour in the mashed garlic and heat till brown. Add the eggplant then stir well till it is well coated with the oil. Reduce heat and let it steam so that the vegetables cook slowly for about 15 minutes. Keep stirring occasionally till cooked.

Once the eggplant is cooked and turns a nice brown color, pour in the paprika and chickpeas, then stir well and let it simmer. Add salt and pepper to taste then simmer for a couple more minutes then serve.

7. Greek Style Zucchini Blossoms with Bulgur

Ingredients

- 3 cloves of garlic
- ½ teaspoon each of pepper and sea salt
- 1 teaspoon of chili pepper
- 1 cup of olive oil
- 1 cup each, chopped onion and chives
- 1 cup of grated zucchini
- 25 zucchini blossoms
- 3 cups of yogurt
- 2/3 cups of raisins
- ½ cup of water

Preparation

Take a deep skillet and pour in about half of the olive oil. Put on the stove on medium heat and sauté the garlic, chives, and onion for 5 minutes. Now add the chili pepper, raisins, bulgur, and zucchini. Then pour in the water and reduce the heat, so the mixture simmers for 10 minutes.

Now turn off the stove then add the mint and pine nuts to the stuffing. Add salt and pepper for seasoning. Use a spoon to stuff each blossom carefully and fold the sides together. Pour in the rest of the olive oil and ½ cup of water. Bake for about 1 hour or until most of the liquid has been absorbed. Serve hot or cold and throw in yogurt if possible.

8. Parsley Salad with Cucumber, Bulgur, and Tomatoes

This is a simple dish with very few ingredients. Always opt for the best and freshest ingredients in the market. Here is a closer look at this dish.

Ingredients

- 1 cup fresh parsley
- 2 tablespoons olive oil
- 1 large red tomato
- ½ cup of tender cucumber
- ½ tablespoon each of salt and pepper

Procedure

Prepare the dressing by chopping up all the vegetables then dicing them into a bowl. Soak the bulgur in the dressing so that it absorbs the flavors. Dice the parsley and add it as a dressing. This mixture can be garnished with herbs such as garlic and others.

9. Homemade Hummus

Humus is a delicious dip and can be used as a side sauce. While there are numerous commercial ones available at grocery stores, it is advisable to prepare your own at home and enjoy it with your favorite dish.

Ingredients

- 400 grams chickpeas
- 1 large lemon juiced
- 3 tablespoons tahini
- ¼ cup of water
- A pinch of paprika
- ½ teaspoon ground cumin
- 2 cloves of minced garlic

- 4 tablespoons of extra virgin olive oil

Directions

Mix lemon juice and tahini in a blender for 1 minute. Add the chickpeas to the blender and mix till completely minced. Now add the olive oil and minced garlic and continue mixing. Blend until the oil is completely soaked in. Add seasoning including cumin and salt then pour 2 tablespoons of water. Let this mixture blend in the machine for one more minute. Add a bit more water if the mixture is too thick.

10. Chicken Tagine with Almonds, Chickpeas, and Apricots

Tagine is the name for both the North African dish and *the vessel in which it's prepared*. The idea is very similar to Western-style braising in Dutch ovens: combine ingredients, cover, and cook over low heat until tender and tasty. The tagine traps steam, creating a very moist cooking environment with even heat.

Ingredients

- 1 teaspoon coriander
- 2 cloves of minced garlic
- 1-inch piece of ginger peeled and minced
- 1 teaspoon of cumin
- 1 carrot peeled and diced
- 1 teaspoon cinnamon
- 1 yellow onion sliced and diced
- 3 pounds of chicken thighs and legs
- 1 cup of dried couscous
- 1 tablespoon honey
- ½ cup of dried and chopped apricots

- ½ cup of dried and chopped almonds

Directions

Warm a tablespoon of oil in an oven over medium heat till the oil is shimmering. Sprinkle salt and pepper on the chicken pieces and place as many pieces as possible. Let this sear for a couple of minutes, 5 – 8 to be precise, flipping occasionally until both sides turn a nice golden brown.

Remove all the chicken pieces to a bowl then put the pan back on the stove with medium heat. Add some olive oil then sauté some carrots and onions. Season these with salt and pepper. Stir until soft then add the garlic. Cook for about 30 seconds and then sprinkle the spices and ginger into the mix.

Add the chicken pieces and apricot into the pan and reduce the heat to low. Bring this mixture to a boil with low heat. While the chicken is cooking, prepare the couscous on the side. Once the chicken is ready, pour it onto a plate. Put the pan back onto the stove and add the chickpeas, almonds, onions, and honey. Add salt and pepper to the stew if necessary.

11. Salmon with Cabbage and Garlic Sandwich

This is a perfect meal for either lunch or dinner. This delicious fish dish is of Greek origin but is now popular around the world. You will enjoy a mild taste of delicious cod with creamy texture and tangy flavors in a soft, toasted sub roll. Here is a simple recipe that you can prepare at home.

Ingredients

- 1 cup of Mojo juice
- ¼ cup olive oil
- 1 head of cabbage diced
- ½ teaspoon of minced garlic
- Brown rolls
- 4 fresh salmon fillets

Mustard Sauce

- 3 teaspoons of Dry Mustard
- 2 teaspoons of Worcester sauce
- Pinch of salt
- 2 tablespoons of whipping cream
- 1 cup of mayo

Procedure

Start by marinating the fish in mojo sauce for about one hour. Next ensure that the cabbaged is nicely chopped and diced to fine slices then set aside. Now mix all the ingredients for the mustard sauce in a small bowl. Refrigerate the bowl with all its contents until required.

After an hour's soaking, the fish fillet should be ready. Put the skillet on the stove and pour in the olive oil. Put the fish fillet in the skillet and add the seasoning. Let it cook until it turns a nice golden-brown color on each side.

Take another skillet then sauté the cabbage with garlic and olive oil. Sauté the cabbage until the cabbage softens, now slice the freshly baked brown toasted slices and spread the sauce evenly on both sides. Place a slice of fish in each and then top it with sautéed cabbage.

12. Chorizo, Mushroom, and Haloumi Tacos

Mushroom, chorizo, and haloumi tacos constitute the tantalizing trio. You can make this dish for a nice summer lunch or even dinner. Tacos are not originally Mediterranean, but haloumi is. This dish takes 20 minutes for preparations and 40 minutes cook time.

Ingredients

- Freshly chopped chilies
- ½ kilo button mushrooms, clean and cut into quarters
- 1 teaspoon salt
- 1 teaspoon black pepper
- 3 tablespoons olive oil
- Chopped coriander
- 8 medium size warm tortillas
- 1 large, cooked sausage sliced into nice chunks

- 200 grams haloumi cheese sliced into two
- A pinch of dried Greek oregano

Preparation

Put the mushroom in a bowl and add the olive oil. Now sprinkle the oregano, sea salt, and pepper. Mix all the ingredients thoroughly and then place on a baking tray. Put this in the oven at 200 degrees C for half an hour then remove from oven and allow it to cool.

Take a pan and pre-heat some olive oil on medium heat. Cook the chorizo for a couple of minutes until it turns crispy then remove it and set aside. Using the same pan fry the haloumi on both side until nice and soft. When ready, remove from the pan and cut into smaller pieces.

Take a spate bowl and use it to combine the chorizo, mushrooms, and haloumi. If you wish to make some tacos, place about 4 tablespoons of mushroom mixture in a hot tortilla. Garnish with coriander and fresh chilies then serve instantly.

13. Louvi – Black Eyed Beans with Chard

Louvi is the name given to black eyed beans in Cyprus. They are perfect for any meal and can be either part of the main meal or side dish. It takes 15 minutes to prepare Louvi and about one hour of cooking time.

Ingredients

- 250 grams of black-eyed beans
- 1 medium sized onion finely diced
- 3 cups or 1 bunch of chard (Silver beet)
- 1 clove of garlic finely chopped
- 1 spring onion diced
- ¼ cup of olive oil
- A pinch of salt
- 2 to 3 tablespoons of finely chopped parsley
- 1 tablespoon of fennel fronds
- 4 cups of water
- ½ cup of lemon juice

Directions

Boil the clack eyed beans in a pot of water for about 15 to 20 minutes. At the same time, was the silver beet and then cut it up into smaller pieces. Take a pan and sauté the garlic and onion with extra virgin olive oil. Add the silver beet and stir.

Now pour the beans into the saucepan and add some salt and pepper. Add some water and lemon juice then cover the saucepan. Let the mixture simmer until it finally boils. Lower heat and let the beans cook on low heat. Remove once the black-eyed beans are soft.

Turn off the heat once the beans get soft then mix in the dill and parsley. The food is now ready to serve so serve with lemon juice and a little bit of olive oil.

14. Braised Okra

Braised okra is a popular Greek dish and a tasty vegetarian dish. It is also very easy to prepare especially because it contains very few ingredients. Okra dishes are almost always vegetarian and include tomatoes and garlic. Using olive oil to braise vegetables this way gives them an additional taste.

Ingredients

- 2 tablespoons red wine vinegar
- ½ kilo fresh okra
- 1 finely chopped onion
- ½ cup of olive oil
- A handful of freshly chopped, flat leaf parsley
- 500 grams of fresh pureed tomatoes
- Salt and pepper to taste

How to Prepare

First clean the okra using water then trim off the pointy ends. Next take the red wine vinegar and sprinkle it on the okra then let it sit for about an hour. After the hour is over, rinse the okra in cold water and then drain.

Take a heavy bottomed sauce pan then heat some olive oil. Sauté the onion on low heat until it turns a nice brown color and soft texture. Once the onions become soft, you should add the okras and the olive oil then let this cook for about five minutes.

Add the parsley and tomatoes then season with pepper and salt to taste. Let this mixture sit on the fire for a short while until it boils. It should boil at possibly 20 to 30 minutes. Once the okra is ready, you should take it off the fire and serve it straight away whilst still hot. Serve with crusty, freshly baked bread.

15. Kale and Lentil Soup

This is a sumptuous recipe that makes use of kale. Kale can be switched with spinach or Swiss chard. Ensure that the vegetables and ingredients are fresh. Here is how to prepare the recipe.

Ingredients

- 3 carrots diced
- 1 onion diced
- 3 celery ribs, sliced
- 1 bay leaf
- 3 garlic cloves diced
- 1/3 cup of flat leaf parsley leaves
- 1 tablespoon of fresh thyme leaves
- 32 ounces of low salt chicken or vegetable broth
- ½ bunch of kale, stemmed, chopped, and rinsed
- 1 cup equivalent to ½ pound of lentils, sorted and rinsed

Preparation method

Take all the ingredients, except for the kale, and mix them in a large pot. Put the pot on a stove on medium to high heat, then cover and leave to boil. Once the mixture boils, stir it for a while then add kale leaves and continue stirring. Continue cooking until the kale wilts and carrots and lentils are tender. This should take a further 10 minutes.

Now puree the soup using an immersion blender. Once the blend is complete, refrigerate in an airtight container for as long as you want. You can also serve it immediately for lunch or dinner.

16. Grilled Fish in Saffron Sauce

Grilled fish is a delightful dish that is pretty easy to make. Grilled fish in Saffron Sauce is of Lebanese origin. You will need whole fish for this recipe. However, if you do not like staring at a fish, then you can find alternatives, like swordfish. It takes 5 minutes to prepare the fish, 10 minutes of cooking time and a further 10 passive minutes.

Ingredients

- 4 fishes, any species common along the Mediterranean area
- 1 pinch of saffron
- ½ cup of olive oil or walnut oil
  1 teaspoon of sea salt
- 1 large lemon or lime sliced into 4 pieces
- ½ cup of tomato sauce or 1 tablespoon of ketchup or tomato paste
- ½ teaspoon of white pepper can be substituted with sumac or cumin

Instructions

Heat your grill oven until it is very hot. As it heats up, season the fish and then brush with oil. Also brush the grill with oil to prevent the fish from sticking. Now put the fish in the grill and leave it there for 3 minutes for each side.

Mix in a small bowl the ingredients of the sauce. Add tomato sauce or paste in order to improve the taste. Brush the fish with the tomato sauce occasionally. Once the fish is nice and crispy, it is ready to eat. Serve whilst hot with lime or lemon quarters.

17. Barbunya Pilaki – Cranberry Beans Cooked with Vegetables

Barbunya Pilaki is a typical Turkish meal that can be served cold as a side dish, or hot as the main dish. Among other things, this meal contains cranberry beans which are known as Borlotti along the Mediterranean.

The beans are cooked in olive oil with carrots, onions, and tomatoes. Pilaki is a Turkish cooking style that means cooking vegetables and beans are cooked with tomato, garlic, and onions on a pan with olive oil.

Ingredients

- 2 cups of dried cranberry (Borlotti) beans soaked overnight in warm water
- 1 finely chopped medium or large onion
- Freshly ground black pepper and salt
- 1 whole lemon split into wedges
- 2 cups of water
- Three tablespoons of olive oil
- A handful of finely chopped flat leaf parsley

- 2 teaspoons of sugar
- 1 can of quality tomatoes chopped
- 2 medium size carrots chopped into small boxes

Procedure

Soak the dried cranberry beans overnight for about 8 hours. Drain the beans the following day, then rinse and put in a container filled with cold water. Put this pot on the stove and bring to a boil.

Now rinse and drain the beans that are already cooled. Set these aside. Take the olive oil and heat it then sauté the onions. Sauté until the color turns brown or onions become soft. Pour in the carrots and sauté for a further two minutes. Season with salt and add some sugar, tomatoes and freshly ground black pepper.

Now let this sauté for about 2 minutes while stirring occasionally. Then add the beans to the pot and mix it thoroughly. Add some water to the mix and then bring it to a boil. Let it simmer on low heat for about half an hour and check the seasoning. Serve whilst hot as the main dish or cold as a side dish.

18. Eggplant Frittata

A frittata is a popular Italian egg-based dish almost similar to an omelet or scrambled eggs. Frittatas are the epitome of summer from the sweet aroma to savory flavors. They constitute a healthy non-meat meal. You can use eggplant to make a frittata. Here is the procedure.

Ingredients

- 700 grams of eggplants peeled and cubed
- 8 free range eggs
- 1 large onion diced
- A tablespoon of chopped parsley
- 2 ounces of grated cheese
- 6 cloves of garlic crushed
- 2 tablespoons of extra virgin olive oil
- Salt and pepper to taste

Procedure

Put the eggplant cubes on a plate and sprinkle some sea salt. Let them sit there for a while. After about 30 minutes, rinse them and pat them dry using paper towels. Take a skillet, add the olive oil and put it on the stove.

Sauté the onion then add the garlic and eggplant cubes. Cook these on medium heat until they turn a nice golden color. Keep stirring them regularly. Take a bowl and whisk the eggs then add the cheese and season with salt and pepper.

Now pour the egg and cheese mixture to the skillet with the cooked eggplants. Pour such that the egg mixture goes to the bottom of the skillet. Cover the skillet and cook on low heat until it is all cooked. Take the chopped parsley and sprinkle on top then serve.

19. Calamari Salad

Calamari salad features crisp bell peppers, tender calamari, and zesty lemon dressing. It is fresh, light, healthy and delicious. While you can eat it right away and it is absolutely delicious, letting it sit for a while to allow the flavors to develop is a better idea.

Ingredients

- 1 Thinly sliced red onion
- 1 Pound of fresh squid rings
- 1 Minced garlic clove
- ½ Pound of mixed baby salad leaves
- ½ Cup of Kalamata olives, halved along the length
- 2 Cups of cherry tomatoes sliced into halves
- 1/3 Cup of extra virgin olive oil
- A splash of red wine vinegar
- 2 tablespoons of freshly squeezed lemon juice

- Freshly ground pepper and salt
- ½ Cup of water

Preparations

Take a bowl and whisk vinegar, lemon juice, garlic, and oil. Add some pepper and salt and stir. Add the onion, stir some more, and then set aside. Take the squid rinks and rinse thoroughly. Boil salted water in an oven then add the squid rings. Cook the squid in the oven, uncovered, for about a minute. Drain in a colander and then put under cold running water for about a minute. Once the squid has cooled, pat it down using paper towels.

Take a large bowl and add salad leaves together with tomatoes and olives. Now add the squid to the salad. Pour in the dressing and mix thoroughly. Check the seasoning and confirm if it is adequate then add some if necessary. If you let the salad sit for a couple of minutes, the flavors will blend nicely, making it even juicier and tastier.

20. Sautéed Greens with Tomatoes and Onions

This is a simple yet perfect recipe for winter. It is popularly known as Tsigareli which is Greek for cabbage with red spicy peppers, fresh tomato, and herbs such as parsley and dill. Here is the preparation process.

Ingredients

- 2.5 Pounds fresh, mixed, and tender greens like dandelion and spinach
- 2 Large onions sliced and diced
- 2 Minced garlic cloves
- ¼ Cup of extra virgin olive oil
- 1.5 Cups of mint leaves or wild fennel leaves
- 2 Leeks washed and finely diced
- 1.5 Cups of snipped fresh dill
- 1 Cup of peel and finely chopped tomatoes

- 2 Teaspoons of sweet paprika powder
- Pepper and salt to taste
- 2 Tablespoons tomato paste
- 1 Teaspoon cayenne pepper

Process

Take the greens and blanch until wilted then drain them thoroughly. Now take a large skillet and heat the olive oil in medium heat. Add the onions and leek and cook until soft, stirring regularly. This should take between 5 to 7 minutes.

Add the cayenne, tomato paste, paprika, and garlic then stir for a couple of minutes. Add the wild fennel leaves, dill, and wilted greens and the tomatoes. Stir for 3 minutes then let it simmer uncovered for about 20 minutes on low heat or until the greens are soft.

By now the dish should be dry so check the seasoning and add salt and cayenne pepper if necessary. The dish is now ready for serving so serve whilst still hot with fresh bread. You can pour some olive oil on the greens once cooked.

Weight Loss and Diet Plan

The Mediterranean diet is more of a lifestyle than a diet. It involves eating nuts and other foods that contain healthy monounsaturated fats. These are good for the heart and keep you feeling fuller. This way, you will eat less and lose weight. When you consume your food, you get most of your nutrition from fiber-rich whole grains like quinoa, barley, oats and brown rice. These foods are natural and non-fattening. They are easily eliminated from the body.

This diet focuses more on fish and seafood and less on red meat. Fish has heart-friendly oils like omega-3 fatty acids. Get rid of red meats and go for tuna, salmon, and sardines. Use olive oil a lot, especially the extra virgin type. This oil is good for your body and has numerous benefits. Add spices and herbs to keep calories down and improve on taste. You do not have to give up on red meat altogether. However, you can have red meat once or twice each month with your meals.

Eat roughly 2000 to 2500 calories of food per day. Half your plate should always consist of a mixture of vegetables. The other half is divided equally so that one side has your protein and the other your carbs. Keeping your portions small and calories low will enable you to lose weight and keep it off.

Conclusion

Thank you for making it through to the end of this book, let's hope it was informative and has provided you with all of the tools you need to achieve your goals whatever they may be.

The next step is to start following this lifestyle. You should come up with your own plan to see how best to implement the Mediterranean diet. It offers a great pathway to healthy eating, great health, weight loss, lower stress, family time, and so much more.

Experts have claimed that this is the best diet and healthiest lifestyle in the world. If you can combine this diet with regular exercise, stress management, and family time, then no doubt you will start cherishing enjoying each and every single day. If you suffer from any chronic conditions, then you can expect to see a great improvement over time. However, if you lack any one of these serious conditions, you can expect this diet and lifestyle to help you stay that way

Finally, if you found this book useful in anyway, a review is always appreciated!

Meal Prep for Beginners:

The Fastest and Most Convenient Cookbook with 50+ Recipes you can get Your Hands on to Prepare Your Meals in a Week Advance to Save Time and Energy! Ready to Go Meals!

Introduction..103

Chapter One: Introduction to Meal Prep............107

Chapter Two: Breakfast Recipes.......................120

Chapter Three: Chicken Recipes......................137

Chapter Four: Red Meat Recipes......................157

Chapter Five: Seafood Recipes........................174

Chapter Six: Vegetable Recipes.......................189

Chapter Seven: Desserts.................................201

Conclusion..219

Introduction

Congratulations on downloading this book, Meal Prep for Beginners: The Fastest and Most Convenient Cookbook with 50+ Recipes you can get Your Hands on to Prepare Your Meals in a Week Advance to Save Time and Energy! Ready to Go Meals!

Meal prepping can be an overwhelming concept, especially if you are just starting out on your fitness journey. I am here to tell you that you are not alone! First off, let me start by congratulating you on making the decision to lead a healthy life. This alone is a very important first step to take. When you decide to put yourself first, the rest of the benefits will follow.

If you are unaware, there are so many incredible benefits to meal prepping. In the chapters to follow, we will be giving you all of the information you need to get started. The very first chapter will bring light to topics such as: what meal prepping is, some helpful examples, and some of my own tips and tricks to make it even easier. As you will soon find out, some of these benefits are for your health, but they also allow you to save and create time to use in more beneficial ways.

In the chapters after the introduction chapter, you will find 50+ delicious recipes. Whether you are looking to prep breakfast or a simple lunch to bring to work with you, this book has got you covered. Within the chapters, you will find seafood recipes, red meat recipes, chicken recipes, and yes, there is even a dessert recipe. I have tried to include a wide selection for it is a common side effect to become bored of the meals prepped at the beginning of the week. By switching it up every once in a while, it will make it easier to stick to your goals and have it be delicious at the same time!

I am so incredibly happy you have decided to start this journey toward a healthier lifestyle. Whether you are looking to lose weight, gain weight, or maintain your current weight, there is a meal prep plan for absolutely everyone. As you will find in the first chapter, it is completely up to you what you feel your meal prep should include. Every individual is different and will have different tastes. I have made it my duty to include a wide array of recipes to match the desires of just about any person. The recipes vary from easy to moderately difficult, so I highly suggest testing out some of our easier recipes as you dip your toes into the meal prepping life.

By the end of this book, I hope you will feel confident in your meal prepping skills. If it doesn't come across easy the first time, I hope you do not give up. If dieting and meal prepping were easy, everyone would do it. You are strong, and you want this change in your life. All it takes is a little bit of time and some dedication. In the first chapter, you will find some weekly plan examples. These are meant to be a guide, not necessarily need to be followed to a T. I do hope you find the answers you are looking for and enjoy the read.

Copyright 2018 by Mia Light - All rights reserved.

The follow eBook is reproduced below with the goal of providing information that is as accurate and reliable as possible. Regardless, purchasing this eBook can be seen as consent to the fact that both the publisher and the author of this book are in no way experts on the topics discussed within and that any recommendations or suggestions that are made herein are for entertainment purposes only. Professionals should be consulted as needed prior to undertaking any of the action endorsed herein.

This declaration is deemed fair and valid by both the American Bar Association and the Committee of Publishers Association and is legally binding throughout the United States.

Furthermore, the transmission, duplication or reproduction of any of the following work including specific information will be considered an illegal act irrespective of if it is done electronically or in print. This extends to creating a secondary or tertiary copy of the work or a recorded copy and is only allowed with express written consent from the Publisher. All additional right reserved.

The information in the following pages is broadly considered to be a truthful and accurate account of facts, and as such any inattention, use or misuse of the information in question by the reader will render any resulting actions solely under their purview. There are no scenarios in which the publisher or the original author of this work can be in any fashion deemed liable for any hardship or damages that may befall them after undertaking information described herein.

Additionally, the information in the following pages is intended only for informational purposes and should thus be thought of as universal. As befitting its nature, it is presented without assurance regarding its prolonged validity or interim quality. Trademarks that are mentioned are done without written consent and can in no way be considered an endorsement from the trademark holder.

Chapter One: Introduction to Meal Prep
What is Meal Prepping?

You are here, reading these words right now because you want to learn how to meal prep. The question is, what is meal prepping? Why is meal prepping a thing and how can it benefit your life? While it may seem overwhelming at first, meal prepping can be fun, easy, and eventually saves you a ton of time! The act of meal prepping is to prepare your meals ahead of time, so you don't have to waste more time of your week, just cooking and eating your meals. Instead, you get the cooking out of the way and bring more focus to what is truly important, your health.

If you want to look at it this way, meal prepping is the healthier version of those TV dinners some people love to buy. However, as opposed to being filled with sodium and who knows what kind of fillers, you will be able to prep healthier and unprocessed ingredients. If this seems like too much work, meal prepping may not be for you. But, if you truly want to change your lifestyle and become healthier, meal prepping is the way to go. Nobody claims you have to put the pedal to the metal and get all of your meal preps. Start out slow! Perhaps this week you only prep your breakfast. As you become more comfortable, you can try and prep lunch for the week after. The best part is, there is no wrong way to meal prep! This journey will be your own to fit your own goals. Whether you are looking to lose weight, gain weight, or maintain your weight, there is a meal prepping plan for you.

Getting Started on Meal Prepping

If you are just starting out, your very first goal is not to be overwhelmed. I have seen too many times where people allow themselves to become dragged down by little details that at the end of the day, don't really matter! The secret is to not incorporate too many things at once. This whole concept is brand new to you. You don't have to be an expert level on day one. This will come in time.

Before we start to meal prep, you need to ask yourself what your own personal goals are. Often times, people go on what we call, "health-kicks," and they go all in. When this happens, more time than not, they will quit after a week! Being healthy is a lifestyle, not a quick fix. You are doing this because you have decided to put yourself and your health first. This is so important to remember! Your results won't happen all at once, it is about the journey to the destination. Up to this point, what have your health choices looked like? If you are shaking your head and saying, not very good, that is okay too. Today is a new day. Today, you are choosing to better yourself and learn all about the meal prepping life. Next, you will learn some easy ways to get started.

Choosing Your Day

To start off, you will want to choose a day where you will prepare your meals. For many individuals, Sunday is one of the best days to begin your meal prepping. For most, this day is one that is off from work, and you can spend the time focusing on your meals. If you have a family, perhaps you can try to get them involved! Health is a lifestyle that can be taught to all ages and carry a lesson to be brought through life.

For those who are a bit more experienced, perhaps you would like two days to prep your meals. One of the most popular options includes Sunday and Wednesday. By choosing these two days, this allows people to split up their week and change up their meals. As I said in the introduction, one of the downfalls of meal prep is that people become sick of eating the same foods. By choosing a couple of days, this allows you to switch up your meals and keep things new and tasty.

If you are a beginner, as we all are at one point or another, I highly suggest not prepping a meal for the whole week. If you are just starting out, let's try to start with no more than perhaps three meals. In my opinion, breakfast is one of the more easy meals to prep. If you are like me, waking up in the morning and cooking is not on top of my list. There are too many things to get done, often times not allotting time for a nutritious breakfast. By meal prepping, all you'll have to do is grab, heat, and go. Who wouldn't take the time to do that?

A handy tool I use for my own meal prepping guide is a calendar. If you are a visual learner like I am, this is the perfect way to organize your meals. Whether you use a real calendar or the one of your cell phone, you will have to find out what works best for you. The most important point is that you choose a day or two that fit your schedule, where you can spend the time you need to prep your meals.

Pick Out Your Meals

Now that you have chosen your day, it is time to decide on the meals you want to prepare. As I said earlier, you may want to focus on breakfast first. If you feel you are ready for a more difficult task, go ahead and set your focus to a lunch or a dinner. If you have a family you are feeding, perhaps you will want to put your efforts toward healthy dinners for the whole family. If you are single, lunches may be more important to you. The best part of meal prepping is how flexible the system is. Take the time to focus on your goals and achieve them the best that you are able to.

When you are picking out your meals, try to focus on creating a balance. Health wise, there are three specific macronutrients you should be focused on. These nutrients include fats, carbohydrates, and proteins. As you will find in the recipe part of the section later, we have included all of this information to help you even more on your fitness journey.

We all have different goals when it comes to our fitness journey. Your micronutrients will change whether you are planning on gaining weight, losing weight, or maintaining. You can use any online calculator to decide what your balanced diet should look like. Once this is determined, this will help you choose out your meals. As a basic guide, your meals should include a protein, a carbohydrate, and a fruit and/or vegetable. Look back on your elementary school food pyramid, and you should have a pretty good idea of how to balance your plate.

An extra tool that may help you out with your macronutrients would be a kitchen scale. If you are trying to lose weight and are counting calories, this would be highly beneficial for you. Speaking of tools, this will bring me to my next important tip to successful meal prepping, your containers.

Meal Prepping Containers

Another tool that will be vital to the success of your meal prepping will be your meal prep containers. Think of these containers as the foundation of your meal prepping. There are a few different factors you will want to take into consideration such as size, sections, and material. These will change depending on not only your situation but also your access. If you find that you do not have access to the containers you are looking for at the store, perhaps try online!

When choosing out your containers, try to find ones that are BPA free. In case you were unaware, BPA stands for bisphenol A, which is a very unhealthy industrial chemical found in certain plastics. By being BPA free, your containers will be microwavable, another very important factor in your meal prepping success. As a suggestion, I typically stick with clear containers so I have easy access to what is in each container.

Overall, there is a simple list for you to follow when you are selecting your containers.

1. Dishwasher Safe
2. Microwave Safe
3. Reusable
4. BPA Free
5. Freezer Safe

Making Your List

To begin, as I already said, it is important to start small. Before you even get to the grocery store, try to pick out your meals and create your grocery list. You can do this on paper, or there are plenty of neat apps on your phone to create the lists on. Either way, planning is the key to success. Once you make this list, you will be able to hit the grocery store and purchase what you need.

Step one is figuring out how many meals you will need. For example, if you are prepping all of your meals for the week, you will need fifteen meals. Instead of cooking fifteen separate dishes, try to create large batches of certain foods to use in various ways. By doing this, you are keeping meal prep simple, and it will be easier on you. Sometimes when recipes include too many ingredients, this causes people to shy away from eating healthy. In the chapters to follow, you will see that the recipes are fairly simple yet delicious.

Remember before you start meal prepping that you will be choosing a day to meal prep. If your day is Sunday, perhaps you can do your big shopping on Saturday or earlier that morning. The key is to be organized. When making your list, keep your grocery store in mind. You will want to try your best to organize your list by section such as meat, dairy, produce, etc. This way, you will be able to zip in and out of the store with no issues or distractions.

Meal Prep Tips and Tricks

I understand that meal prepping can be overwhelming. There are new elements such as new foods, new tools, and new ways of cooking foods. As I said, this book is here to help you every step of the way.

1. Find the Time
   We find excuses, it is just a part of human nature. We find any excuse we can to not put ourselves first. We tell ourselves, I'll do it later, or I just don't have the time. It is important to make the time to put the focus on our health. At the end of the day, you will really only need two or three hours to meal prep. As I said earlier, choose your day and stick to the plan. This is absolutely something you can do!
2. Overlap Ingredients

To make meal prepping a bit easier, try to use ingredients that can overlap and be used in multiple meals. This will save you time and money when you are meal prepping. As you write out your grocery list, think of meals that utilize the same proteins or vegetables. You will thank yourself for making it that much easier by planning ahead.

3. Freezer Friendly

   You may or may not know, but some recipes freeze easier than others. If you plan on prepping your meals for the whole week as opposed to every couple of days, try to cook meals you can pop in the freezer. Some examples of this would be brothers, soups, and smoothies. These are especially good when you are short on time and find yourself tempted with takeout.

4. 1+1+1 Rule

   If you are unsure with where to start with your meal preps, remember the 1+1+1 rule. Essentially, this just means that you will want to have a protein, a carb, and a fresh produce with every meal. Of course, these portions will change depending on what your goals are, but this is a pretty basic plan to follow.

5. Bulk Buy

   Another excuse people use when it comes to meal prepping and eating healthy is that it is just too expensive. Luckily for you, there are ways to save money. When you buy in bulk, it helps lower the price. By doing this, you will be able to cook enough for the week and freeze the rest to be used at a later time.

6. Reflect on Your Goals

   When selecting your recipes, they should reflect your goals. As I said before, you will need to balance your complex carbs, your healthy fats, and your proteins. You will want to do the best you can to avoid refined sugars and artificial sweeteners. Below, you will find a basic list to add to your grocery list

Proteins:

Turkey, chicken, steak, ground beef, tuna, eggs, lentils, tofu, pinto beans, black beans, salmon, shrimp, and chickpeas.

Vegetables:

Spinach, collard greens, kale, squash, peppers, carrots, cauliflower, green beans, mushrooms, asparagus, beets, and broccoli.

Carbohydrates:

Whole wheat bread, whole wheat pasta, brown rice, oats, sweet potatoes, and quinoa.

Healthy Fats

Nut butter, avocado oil, olive oil, coconut oil, cashews, olives, avocado, and almonds.

Fruits:

Apples, blueberries, strawberries, raspberries, blackberries, oranges, pineapple, melon, mangoes, and bananas.

Of course, this isn't a complete list. The best part of meal prepping is how customizable it is. All you have to do is take the time to sit down and decide what your goals are. Are you looking to lose weight? Perhaps you would like to gain some weight? No matter what, you can choose the foods you want to consume and go from there!

Meal Prep Pros and Cons

Just like with any diet, meal prepping just isn't for everyone! But, you are here for a reason, right? Below, I will list just some of the pros and cons that come with meal prepping. After, you can decide if this lifestyle would be best for you.
Pros:

1. Free Time
   At this point, you understand that meal prepping is meant to save you time. Indeed, once all of your cooking is done, you will have the rest of your week to do as you please! You will have no excuse to eat unhealthy because it will already be made! By prepping your meals, time will be one less thing you have to worry about.
2. Thoughtful Meals
   The whole point of meal prepping is to eat healthier. By taking the time to sit down and create your meals at the beginning of the week, you are taking the time to put your health first. By planning, you won't have the time or thought to opt for an easier, less healthy meal.
3. Portion Controls
   If you are looking to lose weight, meal prep will be one of your essential goals. Sometimes when people cook their meals, they throw any sense of portion control out the window. When you are meal prepping, you become more aware of portions as only a certain amount of food can fit into your containers in the first place!
4. Decrease Temptation
   We have all been there. Perhaps driving home or laying on the couch, you think about how much easier it would be to order out or drive through somewhere instead of

taking the time to cook. I understand it can be incredibly tempting. However, when you meal prep, it is like a healthier version of takeout!

5. Saving Money

   As I mentioned before, meal prepping is a great way to save money. First off, you can buy in bulk to help lower the price of the foods you are buying. You will also be saving money by not eating out all of the time! Often times, we are not aware of it, but we do spend a lot of money out, just because of the convenience. Why not make your meals more convenient and healthy at the same time!

Cons

1. Exhausting

   Cooking isn't for everyone, I understand that. It can be tiring to spend a few hours in the kitchen cooking up your meals. Meal prepping is going to take time and effort, there is no getting around that. This is just another reason I suggest choosing a day where you can take your time with meal prepping. It will take some time to shop, cook, and clean the dishes after. Who says you need to rush? As long as you anticipate the time needed, there is no need to feel exhausted by meal prepping.

2. Bored

   Eating the same meals during the week can be incredibly boring. This is especially true if you plan a meal and just don't feel like eating that particular food that day. This is why I suggest prepping multiple meals during the week. You will want to choose recipes that you can get excited over. If you feel that you are forcing yourself to eat a meal, there is no way you will

stick to the lifestyle. You are in charge of what you are eating and cooking, choose wisely!
3. Portion Control
There is a popular term circulating society known as HANGRY. You know, that feeling you get when you are just so hungry that you get mad. If you are looking to lose weight, you may experience this with meal prepping. As you meal prep, you will be focused on making your portions smaller. As a suggestion, I will tell you to decrease your serving sizes slowly. You will need to shrink your stomach so it can get used to smaller portions. If you dive right into it, you will increase your desire to overeat. Avoid this and start slow as I keep suggesting.

Choosing a Plan

We are all here for different reasons. Some are looking to save time, others looking to eat healthier. Whether you are looking to lose weight or gain weight, there are different ways to look at your meal prepping. One way to look at it is to count calories. We suggest planning your meals depending on your macronutrients. This way, you can plan specific foods for your meals without having to count all of those calories. You will want to use an online calculator to decide what your macronutrients will look like. Here is the basic information you will need:

1. Age
2. Sex
3. Height
4. Weight

5. Goal (Fat Loss, Muscle Gain, Maintenance)
6. Activity Level (Light, Moderate, Active)

By using the information above, a calculator can give you the macronutrients to meet your goal. Once this is determined, you can go ahead and choose your meals for the week. As a basic recommended macronutrient ratio, it is recommended to have 35% protein, 25% carbohydrates, and 40% fats. As discussed, these numbers will change depending on your health goals.

Meal Prep Examples:
Breakfast M/W/F: Oat and Jam Muffins
Breakfast T/Thu: Detox Ginger and Peach Smoothie
Lunch M/W/F: Tangy Lemon Thyme Chicken
Lunch T/Thu: Easy Turkey Chili
Dinner M/W/F: Crusted Herb Pork Chops + Garlic Roasted Cauliflower
Dinner M/W/F: Spicy Moroccan Salmon + Cilantro and Lime Cauliflower Rice

Breakfast M/W/F: Oatmeal Carrot Cake Breakfast Bars
Breakfast T/Thu: CPK Smoothie
Lunch M/W/F: Zesty Lime and Cilantro Chicken Tacos
Lunch T/Thu: Spicy Crab Stuffed Cucumber Cups
Dinner M/W/F: Slow Cooker Tomato and Beef Stew
Dinner T/ Thu: Pesto and Tomato Chicken Rolls + Simple Roasted Asparagus

Breakfast M/W/F: Sweet Apple Cider Oatmeal Breakfast
Breakfast T/Thu: Banana and Oat Breakfast Smoothie
Lunch M/W/F: One Pan Cashew and Chicken Stir Fry

Lunch T/Thu: Sweet and Spicy Glazed Sriracha Meatballs + Roasted Butternut Squash
Dinner M/W/F: Grilled Onion and Peppers Tilapia Tacos
Dinner T/Thu: Baked Taco Pie

Breakfast M/W/F: Veggie Eggie Breakfast Muffins
Breakfast T/Thu: Oat and Strawberry Jam Muffins
Lunch M/W/F: Chicken Bruschetta
Lunch T/Thu: Avocado and Spicy Tuna Wrap
Dinner M/W/F: Jerk Caribbean Shrimp + Lemon and Garlic Roasted Broccoli
Dinner M/W/F: Spicy Sausage Spaghetti Squash Ships

    As for snacks and desserts, feel free to sprinkle these in as needed. It is important to stick to your calorie goal but also allow yourself a treat every once in a while. If you don't, you run a higher risk of eating more of the bad foods you are craving.

Chapter Two: Breakfast Recipes
Mixed Berry Slow Cooker Breakfast Quinoa

Eight Servings
Serving Size: One Cup
Carbohydrates: 44g
Proteins: 7g
Fats: 3g
Ingredients:

- Vanilla Extract (2 t.)
- Maple Syrup (2 T.)
- Cinnamon (1 t.)
- Salt (.15 t.)
- Mixed Berries (2 C.)
- Quinoa (2 C.)

- Water (4 C.)
- Bananas (2)

Directions:

1. To start off, you will want to take your slow cooker and coat it with your cooking spray of choice. Once it is covered, toss in all of the ingredients from the list above.
2. Once the ingredients have been placed, turn your slow cooker on low and allow this mixture to cook for five to six hours.
3. For additional flavors, add in your favorite nuts or fruit! Spoon a cup into each container and store in the fridge for a quick and easy breakfast.

Veggie Eggie Breakfast Muffins
Twelve Servings
Serving Size: One Muffin
Carbohydrates: 3g
Proteins: 5g
Fats: 5g
Ingredients:

- Arugula (2 C.)
- Red Bell Pepper (1)
- Eggs (8)
- Garlic (2 Cloves)
- Onion (.5)
- Olive Oil (1 T.)
- Parmesan Cheese (.25 C.)
- Salt & Pepper (Pinch)

Directions:

1. You will want to start off by heating your oven to 375 degrees.
2. As your oven heats up, take a muffin tin and spray it with your cooking spray of choice.
3. In a medium pan, begin to heat up your tablespoon of olive oil. When the olive oil begins to sizzle, toss in your onion and garlic and cook for five minutes or so. Once these are cooked, you can also throw in your bell peppers.
4. When all of your vegetables are cooked, chop them up and place into the bottom of each muffin tin.

5. In a bowl, whisk your cheese, arugula, and eggs all together. If desired, you can take this time to season the eggs with salt and pepper.
6. When the egg mixture is ready, go ahead and pour it evenly into each muffin hole. Be sure not to overfill the tins as the eggs will rise slightly during the cooking process.
7. Finally, pop the tin in for about twenty minutes. This should be enough time to cook through.
8. When they are done, allow them to cool and place each egg muffin into a container for an easy to go breakfast muffin.

Oat and Strawberry Jam Muffins

Twelve Servings
Serving Size: One Muffin
Carbohydrates: 21g
Proteins: 5g
Fats: 4g
Ingredients:

- Strawberry Jam (.25 C.)
- Vanilla Extract (1 t.)
- Honey (1 T.)
- Coconut Oil (2 T.)
- Almond Milk (1 C.)
- Eggs (2)
- Stevia (.50 C.)
- Baking Powder (1 T.)
- Oat Flour (.50 C.)
- Whole Wheat Flour (2 C.)

Directions:

1. Start off by heating your oven to 425 degrees.
2. As the oven heats up, take out a small bowl and use a flour sifter to sift through your oat flour, whole wheat flour, and the baking powder.
3. Once this is in place, you will want to toss in your half cup of stevia and mix everything together.
4. In a different bowl, mix together the almond milk, melted coconut oil, eggs, vanilla extract, and the honey.
5. Now, pour the wet ingredients over your dry ingredients and mix everything together.

6. Next, you will want to take a greased muffin tin pan and spoon the batter between each one of the holes.
7. When the muffin tins are filled, go ahead and teaspoon the strawberry jam on top of the batter. Using a toothpick, you will want to swirl the ingredients together. For a lower calorie option, try sugar-free jam in your muffins.
8. Once the muffins are ready, toss them into the oven for twenty minutes. They will be ready when you are able to stick a toothpick in the middle, and it comes out clean.
9. When done, remove muffins from the oven and allow them to cool.

Sweet and Spicy Sweet Potato Hash Browns
Two Servings
Serving Size: .5 C.
Carbohydrates: 30g
Proteins: 3g
Fats: 8g
Ingredients:

- Chili Powder (.15 t.)
- Cinnamon (.15 t.)
- Salt (.50 t.)
- Butter (3 T.)
- Onion (.50 C.)
- Sweet Potatoes (2)
- Black Pepper (Pinch)

Directions:

1. You will want to start off by preparing your sweet potatoes. You can do this by peeling and shredding the sweet potatoes with a grater. Be sure to squeeze any excess water out, as this may mess up the recipe.
2. Once your sweet potato is prepared, take a skillet and begin to melt the butter from the list above. Once the butter is melted, toss in your onion and cook for a total of two minutes. Season the mixture with the chili powder, salt, pepper, and cinnamon.
3. When the onion is cooked through, add in your grated sweet potato. Allow this mixture to cook for five to eight minutes. It is cooked through once it becomes a browned color.

4. When it begins to brown, flip the sweet potato mixture over and be sure to cook the other side for around five minutes or so.
5. Once both sides are cooked, portion the sweet potatoes into your containers and enjoy with a piece of fruit or perhaps an egg muffin from the recipe above!

Oatmeal Carrot Cake Breakfast Bars

Sixteen Servings
Serving Size: One Bar
Carbohydrates: 16g
Proteins: 4g
Fats: 6g
Ingredients:

- Carrots (.50, grated)
- Vanilla Extract (1 t.)
- Maple Syrup (.50 C.)
- Coconut Oil (.25 C.)
- Soy Milk (1 C.)
- Egg (1)
- Nutmeg (.15 t.)
- Cinnamon (2 t.)
- Baking Powder (1 t.)
- Rolled Oats (2.50 C.)

Directions:

1. Start off by heating your oven to 350 degrees.
2. While the oven is heating up, take a bowl and mix together your nutmeg, cinnamon, baking powder, and oats. If desired, you can toss in some salt, but it is not needed.

3. In another bowl, whisk together your coconut oil, maple syrup, vanilla, eggs, and milk.
4. Once both are prepared, you can mix together your wet and dry ingredients in the same bowl.
5. Now that you have your mixture, you can pour it into a greased baking dish.
6. Pop this dish in your heated oven for a total of forty minutes.
7. Remove the dish from the oven, allow to cool, and slice into bars for easy, on the go breakfast bars!

Overnight Oats Blueberry Muffin Style
One Serving
Serving Size: One Jar
Carbohydrates: 41g
Proteins: 14g
Fats: 6g
Ingredients:

- Blueberries (.25 C.)
- Vanilla Extract (1 t.)
- Cinnamon (.15 t.)
- Honey (.50 T.)
- Chia Seeds (1 T.)
- Almond Milk (.33 C.)
- Greek Yogurt (.33 C.)
- Rolled Oats (.33 C.)

Directions:

1. Take a jar or a bowl and place your yogurt, chia seeds, honey, vanilla, cinnamon, and oats all together.
2. Once everything is well combined, cover the jar/bowl with plastic wrap and pop it into the fridge overnight.
3. When you are ready to enjoy your meal, cover with fresh blueberries, and you have a quick and healthy meal!

Sweet Apple Cider Oatmeal Breakfast
Eight Servings
Serving Size: .75 C.
Carbohydrates: 43g
Proteins: 4g
Fats: 10g
Ingredients:

- Cinnamon Sticks (2)
- Maple Syrup (.33 C.)
- Apple Cider (2 C.)
- Apples (6)

Topping Ingredients:

- Allspice (.50 t.)
- Cinnamon (1 t.)
- Vanilla Extract (1 t.)
- Apple Cider Mix (.25 C.)
- Almond Flour (.50 C.) + (2 T.)
- Pecans (.50 C.)
- Rolled Oats (1 C.)

Directions:

1. To begin, you will want to heat your oven to 375 degrees.
2. While this is heating up, go ahead and prep your apples by washing, peeling and slicing them. Once they are done, set them aside in a bowl.
3. Over medium heat, bring a small saucepan with the apple cider, maple syrup, and cinnamon to a boil. Once it is boiling, turn the heat lower and allow this mixture to simmer for around twenty minutes. Now, the liquid should

be reduced, and you can pour this mixture over your apples. Be sure to reserve .25 C. of this liquid for later use.
4. In another bowl, mix together your pecans, almond flour, apple cider mixture, cinnamon, salt, allspice, vanilla, and the rolled oats.
5. Now that these are ready, place the apples into a baking dish and sprinkle the above mixture over the top.
6. Pop the dish into your oven for thirty minutes. By the end, your apples should be tender and delicious.
7. Spoon the mixture into ¾ cups into your containers and breakfast will be ready for you when you want it!

CPK Smoothie

Two Servings
Serving Size: 1 C.
Carbohydrates: 41g
Proteins: 8g
Fats: 5g
Ingredients:

- Chia Seeds (2 T.)
- Orange Juice (.25 C.)
- Pineapple (.25 C.)
- Greek Yogurt (.50 C.)
- Banana (1)
- Kiwi (1 C.)
- Spinach (2 C.)

Directions:

1. First, you will want to prepare all of the ingredients from above. Be sure they are washed, peeled, and chopped into smaller pieces.
2. Once this is done, toss them into a blender and blend for thirty seconds or until they are well combined.
3. Divide your smoothie into proper portions and store until ready to be served for a quick and easy breakfast idea.

Banana and Oat Breakfast Smoothie

Two Servings
Serving Size: 1 C.
Carbohydrates: 33g
Proteins: 6g
Fats: 8g
Ingredients:

- Almond Milk (.50 C.)
- Cinnamon (.50 t.)
- Flaxseed Meal (1 T.)
- Banana (1)
- Yogurt (.50 C.)
- Rolled Oats (.33 C.)

Directions:

1. Begin by preparing the banana. Be sure it is washed, peeled, and chopped into smaller pieces.
2. Toss all of the ingredients from the list above into a blender and blend for thirty seconds or until everything is well combined.
3. Separate the smoothie into two servings and breakfast is ready.

Detox Ginger and Peach Smoothie

Two Servings
Serving Size: .50 C.
Carbohydrates: 27g
Proteins: 6g
Fats: .5g
Ingredients:

- Coconut Water (1 C.)
- Stevia (1 Packet)
- Greek Yogurt (.25 C.)
- Ginger (1 T.)
- Banana (.50)
- Peaches (2 C.)
- Spinach (1 C.)

Directions:

1. Take all of the ingredients from the list above and toss them into your blender.
2. Blend for thirty seconds or until everything is well combined. For a thicker smoothie, try adding in ice.
3. Finally, portion out your smoothie and breakfast is ready.

Homemade Nut Bar

Ten Servings
Serving Size: One Bar
Carbohydrates: 18g
Proteins: 5g
Fats: 12g
Ingredients:

- Dark Chocolate Chips (.50 C.)
- Salt (.50 t.)
- Vanilla Extract (.50 t.)
- Honey (2 T.)
- Brown Rice Syrup (.25 C.)
- Flaxseed Meal (1 T.)
- Puffed Rice (.33 C.)
- Walnuts (.50 C.)
- Dry Roasted Peanuts (.50 C.)
- Dry Roasted Almonds (.50 C.)

Directions:

1. Begin by lining a pan with aluminum foil so that it is prepared for this recipe.
2. Now, take a small bowl and mix together the flaxseed meal, puffed rice, and the nuts.
3. In a saucepan, bring the following to a boil: salt, vanilla, honey, and brown rice syrup. Continue to stir this mixture for two minutes or so.
4. When this is done, pour the wet ingredients over the nuts and combine everything.

5. Place this mixture into the bottom of the pan and be sure to spread it out evenly so that there are no gaps.
6. Pop the dish into the fridge and allow it to cool for twenty to thirty minutes or until solid.
7. For a finishing touch, go ahead and melt the chocolate chips. Carefully drizzle the chocolate over the mixture and then cut them into bars.
8. Portion out your bars, and you have an easy to grab breakfast!

Chapter Three: Chicken Recipes
Tangy Lemon Thyme Chicken

Four Servings
Serving Size: One Chicken Breast
Carbohydrates: 3g
Proteins: 25g
Fats: 4g
Ingredients:

- Thyme (1 T.)
- Salt (1 t.)
- Pepper (.50 t.)
- Lemon (1-Zest)
- Lemons (2-Juice)
- Chicken Breast (4)

Directions:

1. Start out by heating your oven to 375 degrees.
2. While this is warming up, take a small bowl and mix together your lemon zest, lemon juice, salt, pepper, and the thyme.
3. When you are ready, place the chicken breast into the bottom of a baking dish and pour the lemon mixture over the top. Be sure to swirl the dish around to assure the chicken is completely coated.
4. Finally, pop the dish into the oven for forty minutes or so. When it is cooked through, the juices will run clear. Once cooked, remove from the oven, cool, and portion one breast per container. For a well-rounded meal, pair with a favorite veggie.

Chicken Bruschetta

Four Servings

Serving Size: One Chicken Breast and .33 C. of Bruschetta

Carbohydrates: 8g

Proteins: 28g

Fats: 4g

Ingredients:

- Basil (.25 C.)
- Salt (.10 t.)
- Balsamic Vinegar (1 t.)
- Olive Oil (1 t.)
- Red Onion (.50)
- Garlic (1)
- Tomatoes (5)
- Chicken Breast (4)

Directions:

1. Begin by heating your oven to 375 degrees.
2. If you desire, season the chicken breast with salt and pepper before popping it onto a baking sheet. Place the chicken in the oven for about forty minutes.
3. While the chicken bakes, take a small bowl and mix together your basil, balsamic vinegar, olive oil, onion, garlic, and the chopped tomatoes.
4. Finally, remove your chicken from the oven and allow to cool. Portion out your chicken into your containers, and you have a very healthy lunch or dinner.

Herb and Balsamic Maple Chicken
Four Servings
Serving Size: One Chicken Breast
Carbohydrates: 10g
Proteins: 27g
Fats: 10g
Ingredients:

- Olive Oil (2 T.)
- Cayenne Pepper (1 t.)
- Garlic (2)
- Dijon Mustard (1 T.)
- Maple Syrup (2 T.)
- Balsamic Vinegar (.25 C.)
- Chicken Breast (4)
- Salt (.50 t.)
- Pepper (.50 t.)

Directions:

1. To begin, you will be making your marinate. This will take thirty minutes, but for better flavor, it is suggested to soak the chicken overnight. Create this mixture by blending the maple syrup, mustard, balsamic vinegar, thyme, salt, pepper, cayenne, and garlic all together. Once this is done, pour over your chicken and allow to oak.
2. When the chicken is seasoned as desired, place in a skillet over medium heat with some olive oil. Cook each side of the chicken for eight minutes or until it is cooked through. Once one side turns a golden-brown color, cook the other side for another eight minutes.

3. Portion out the chicken to your containers and eat with a delicious vegetable for a well-rounded meal.

Quinoa Chicken Fajita Soup in Slow Cooker
Six Servings
Serving Size: 1.50 C.
Carbohydrates: 50g
Proteins: 30g
Fats: 5g
Ingredients:

- Salt (2 t.)
- Paprika (2 t.)
- Cumin (1 T.)
- Chili Powder (1.50 T.)
- Corn (1 C.)
- Black Beans (1 Can)
- Green Chiles (1 Can)
- Diced Tomatoes (1 Can)
- Lime (1-Juice)
- Low-sodium Chicken Broth (4 C.)
- Garlic (3)
- Onion (1)
- Bell Peppers (3)
- Quinoa (1 C.)
- Chicken Breast (1.50 Lbs.)

Directions:

1. The best part of the slow cooker is being able to toss all of the ingredients from above into it and forgetting about it. If you need a quick meal, toss all of the ingredients on high for four hours. For a slower cook, put the mixture on a low heat for eight hours.

2. Once the chicken is cooked through, turn the heat off and allow to cool. You will want to take two forks and gently shred the chicken. If you want, go ahead and season with salt and pepper to taste.
3. Finally, portion out your soup and you have a quick meal for lunch or dinner.

One Pan Tangy Rosemary Chicken with Potatoes
Four Servings
Serving Size: One Chicken Breast, .50 C. Potatoes, .25 C. Green Beans
Carbohydrates: 26g
Proteins: 39g
Fats: 3g
Ingredients:

- Green Beans (1 Lb.)
- Red Potatoes (3 C.)
- Chicken Breast (4)
- Black Pepper (1 t.)
- Salt (1 t.)
- Thyme (1 T.)
- Rosemary (1 T.)
- Garlic (2)
- Lemon (1-Zest)
- Lemon Juice (1 T.)
- Olive Oil (3 T.)

Directions:

1. Start off this recipe by heating your oven to 400 degrees.
2. While this warms up, take a small bowl and mix together the olive oil, lemon zest, lemon juice, thyme, pepper, salt, and the rosemary.

3. In a different bowl, mix together the baby potatoes with a tablespoon of olive oil. If you would like, you can also add some salt and pepper to this recipe as desired.
4. Now that these are ready, take a large baking dish and arrange your chicken and green beans on it. Once in place, also put the potatoes on the sheet.
5. Finally, drizzle the mixture from above and be sure all of the ingredients are evenly coated.
6. When you are ready, toss the sheet into the oven for thirty minutes or so. When you pull it out, the chicken should be cooked through, and the green beans will be crisp.
7. Once cooked, portion out the ingredients from above and enjoy!

One Pan Cashew and Chicken Stir Fry
Six Servings
Serving Size: 1 C.
Carbohydrates: 18g
Proteins: 21g
Fats: 3g
Ingredients:

- Unsalted Cashews (.33 C.)
- Green Onions (4)
- Carrots (.50 C.)
- Sugar Snap Peas (1 C.)
- Red Bell Pepper (1)
- Broccoli (2 C.)
- Chicken Breast (1 Lb.)
- Olive Oil (1 T.)
- Garlic (3)

Sauce:

- Water (3 T.)
- Ginger (1 T.)
- Sesame Oil (1 t.)
- Honey (2 T.)
- Peanut Butter (3 T.)
- Soy Sauce (4 T.)

Directions:

1. To begin, you will start by making the sauce for this recipe. You can do so by taking a small bowl and mixing together the water, ginger, sesame oil, honey, peanut

butter, and the soy sauce. You can add more water for a thinner sauce.
2. Once this is done, begin to heat the olive oil in a medium size pan over medium heat. Once the olive oil is sizzling, add in your chicken and cook on either side. This should take ten minutes or so. Once cooked through, season with garlic, salt, and the pepper.
3. When you feel the chicken is cooked through, you can add in the broccoli, snap peas, bell pepper, and carrots and allow them to cook. This should take an extra five minutes.
4. Now that all of your ingredients are cooked, drizzle the sauce over and be sure to coat everything evenly.
5. Finally, add in your cashews as a final touch. Portion out the meal, and you have a delicious lunch or dinner for the week!

Zesty Lime and Cilantro Chicken Tacos
Five Servings
Serving Size: Two Tacos
Carbohydrates: 60g
Proteins: 36g
Fats: 20g
Ingredients:

- Whole Wheat Tortillas (10)
- Chicken (1.50 Lbs.)

Marinade:

- Cilantro (2 T.)
- Honey (.50 t.)
- Garlic (2)
- Olive Oil (1 T.)
- Lime (2-Juice)
- Lime (1-Zest)

Topping Coleslaw:

- Honey (1 t.)
- Olive Oil (1 T.)
- Lime (2)
- Green Onion (.50 C.)
- Cilantro (.50 C.)
- Carrots (1 C.)
- Red Cabbage (1 C.)
- Green Cabbage (2 C.)

Directions:

1. Begin by making your marinade. You will do this by mixing together the cilantro, honey, garlic, olive oil, lime zest, and lime juice. When it is combined, toss in your chicken and allow it to soak for four hours or best, overnight.
2. In the meantime, you can make the coleslaw by first, shredding the cabbages and carrots. Mix these together with the olive oil, honey, and lime juice.
3. Once the chicken is seasoned properly, take a medium pan over medium heat and cook the chicken for five minutes on either side. Be sure that the chicken is cooked through.
4. When you are ready to prep your meals, place the chicken into the tortillas and top with the coleslaw.

Sweet Hawaiian Pineapple and Chicken Kabobs
Five Servings
Serving Size: 2 Skewers
Carbohydrates: 21g
Proteins: 26g
Fats: .2g
Ingredients:

- Pineapple (3 C.)
- Onion (1)
- Bell Peppers (3)
- Chicken Breast (1.25 Lbs.)

Marinade:

- Garlic (2)
- Grated Ginger (2 t.)
- Hot Chili Paste (1 T.)
- Olive Oil (1 T.)
- Honey (1 T.)
- Soy Sauce (.25 C.)
- Pineapple Juice (.25 C.)

Directions:

1. Start off by making your marinade for the chicken. Do this by taking the ingredients from above and mixing it all together in a small to a medium-sized bowl. When this is done, pour it over your chicken and allow it to soak for at least an hour. When pouring over your chicken, save .25 C. of the marinade for later use.
2. Once the chicken is ready, prepare the bell peppers, pineapple, and onion by cutting them into smaller chunks.

When this is done, go ahead and place a skewer through the ingredients to create your kabobs.
3. When this is done, place the kebobs on the grill or oven for four to five minutes on each side. If you want, brush the marinade you reserved from earlier over the kabobs to keep them moist.
4. Finally, portion out the skewers and try with a delicious quinoa side.

Pesto and Tomato Chicken Rolls

Six Servings
Serving Size: One Chicken Roll
Carbohydrates: 14g
Proteins: 42g
Fats: 17g
Ingredients:

- Crushed Tomatoes (1 Can)
- Mozzarella Cheese (.50 C.)
- Egg (1)
- Shredded Cheese (.25 C.)
- Garlic Powder (.50 t.)
- Oregano (1 t.)
- Flaxseed Meal (2 T.)
- Whole Wheat Panko Breadcrumbs (.50 C.)
- Chicken Breast (6)
- Salt (.50 t.)
- Pepper (.50 t.)

Pesto Sauce:

- Salt (.50 t.)
- Pepper (.50 t.)
- Basil Leaves (1 C.)
- Parmesan Cheese (1 C.)
- Garlic (3)
- Tomatoes (1 Jar)

Directions:

1. To begin, you will want to heat your oven to 375 degrees.

2. Now, as this heats up, make the pesto sauce. You will do this by adding the pesto sauce ingredients from the list above and pulsing in a food processor. Once this is done, put the sauce to the side.
3. Now, you will need a meat tenderizer to flatten your chicken breast to about .25 in. thick. Once this is done, season it with salt and pepper and spread your fresh made pesto onto the chicken. For a final touch, sprinkle in the shredded cheese and roll the chicken up. You can secure this with the help of a toothpick.
4. In a small bowl, add in the garlic powder, oregano, flaxseed meal, and breadcrumbs.
5. In another bowl, mix together the egg with a couple tablespoons of water.
6. When you are ready, dip the rolled chicken into the egg mixture and coat the chicken with the breadcrumbs.
7. Once this is complete, place the chicken rolls onto a sheet and cook for thirty minutes in the oven.
8. Finally, remove the chicken, place mozzarella over the top and cook for another five minutes to allow the cheese to melt.
9. Portion out the chicken rolls into your containers, and you have a delicious, ready to go meal.

Ginger and Turmeric Grilled Chicken

Four Servings
Serving Size: One Chicken Breast
Carbohydrates: 3g
Proteins: 48g
Fats: 10g
Ingredients:

- Lime Juice (1 T.)
- Salt (.50 t.)
- Pepper (.50 t.)
- Cumin (.50 t.)
- Coriander (1 t.)
- Ginger (1 T.)
- Turmeric (1 t.)
- Garlic (2)
- Olive Oil (1 T.)
- Coconut Milk (.50 Can)

- Chicken Breast (4)

Directions:

1. Begin by mixing together your marinade. Do this by taking a small bowl and mixing together the salt, pepper, lime juice, coriander, ginger, turmeric, garlic, olive oil, and coconut milk.
2. Pour this mixture over the chicken and allow it to marinade for at least one hour. If you have the time, allow this to soak overnight for maximum flavor.
3. When the chicken is ready, place it in a medium pan over medium heat and cook for five or six minutes on either side.
4. For extra flavor, squeeze some fresh lime juice over the chicken.
5. Portion the chicken out and enjoy with your favorite vegetable or rice.

Thin Chicken Pot Pie

Five Serving
Serving Size: One Pie
Carbohydrates: 36g
Proteins: 24g
Fats: 4g
Ingredients:

- Reduced-fat Biscuits (1 Can)
- Pepper (.25 t.)
- Salt (1 t.)
- Green Onions (4)
- Mixed Frozen Vegetables (1 Package)
- Chicken Breast (2 C.)
- Thyme (1 t.)
- Poultry Seasoning (1 t.)
- All-purpose Flour (3 T.)
- Fat-free Chicken Broth (1 C.)
- Half and Half (1 C.)

Directions:

1. Start off by heating your oven to 425 degrees.
2. While this is heating up, you will want to bring the following ingredients to a boil: thyme, poultry seasoning, flour, chicken broth, and the half and half. Once it is boiling, reduce the heat and allow the ingredients to simmer for about four minutes.
3. Once this mixture becomes thick, remove it from the heat and mix in the salt, pepper, green onion, veggies, and chicken.

4. Next, roll out your biscuits and put them into greased muffin tins.
5. Place the biscuit and fill the cup with the chicken filling. Once it is filled, cover up the cups and pierce holes into the top.
6. Pop these into the oven for twelve to fifteen minutes.
7. Remove from oven once the biscuits are golden and they are ready to enjoy!

Chapter Four: Red Meat Recipes
Crusted Herb Pork Chops

Four Servings
Serving Size: One Pork Chop
Carbohydrates: 5g
Proteins: 25g
Fats: 10g
Ingredients:

- Olive Oil (1 T.)
- Pepper (.50 t.)
- Salt (.50 t.)
- Parsley (1 T.)
- Thyme (1 T.)
- Panko Breadcrumbs (.50 C.)
- Dijon Mustard (2 T.)
- Pork Chops (4)

Directions:

1. Begin by heating your oven to 450 degrees.
2. Next, you will prep your pork chops by rubbing them with the Dijon mustard.
3. In a small bowl, combine the salt, pepper, parsley, thyme, and panko breadcrumbs. For a healthier version, try to get whole wheat breadcrumbs.
4. When you are ready, dip the mustard covered pork chops into the breadcrumbs. Be sure that they are coated evenly.
5. Once they are ready, go ahead and heat a large skillet over medium heat and put your olive oil in. Sauté the chop for two or three minutes on each side before popping it into the oven.
6. Keep the pork chops in the oven for eight to ten minutes before removing and allowing to cool. Portion into your containers and serve with your favorite side.

Spicy Sausage Spaghetti Squash Ships
Four Servings
Serving Size: One Boat
Carbohydrates: 17g
Proteins: 22g
Fats: 14g
Ingredients:

- Basil (2 T.)
- Mozzarella Cheese (.50 C.)
- Pepper (.50 t.)
- Salt (.50 t.)
- Half and Half (.25 C.)
- Tomatoes (1 Can)
- Chicken Broth (1 C.)
- Turkey Sausage (1 Lb.)
- Garlic (1)
- Onion (1)
- Olive Oil (1 T.)
- Spaghetti Squash (2)

Directions:

1. To start, you will be heating your oven to 350 degrees.
2. While this heats up, it is time to prepare your squash. Do this by cutting it down the middle and removing the seeds. Once you have done this, go ahead and place on a baking sheet and stick in the oven for forty-five minutes.
3. As the squash cooks, bring the tablespoon of olive oil to a sizzle in a skillet over medium heat. Once it is, add in the onion, garlic, and turkey sausage until it is cooked

through. Once this happens, you can add in the salt, pepper, half and half, tomatoes and the chicken broth.
4. Now that the squash is cooked, remove from the oven and allow it to cool for a bit. When you can, shred the squash with two forks and remove into a bowl. In this bowl, mix together the spaghetti squash with the cheese and put it back into the bowl with the other mixture.
5. If desired, top with more cheese and pop it into the oven to melt the cheese. Top with basil and your meal is ready!

Sweet and Spicy Glazed Sriracha Meatballs

Eight Servings
Serving Size: Five Meatballs
Carbohydrates: 19g
Proteins: 27g
Fats: 11
Ingredients:

- Black Pepper (.50 t.)
- Salt (.50 t.)
- Garlic Powder (.50 t.)
- Green Onion (.25 C.)
- Eggs (2)
- Panko Breadcrumbs (1 C.)
- Ground Turkey (2 Lbs.)

Sauce:

- Toasted Sesame Oil (.50 t.)
- Garlic (3)
- Ginger (1 T.)
- Honey (3 T.)
- Rice Vinegar (3 T.)
- Soy Sauce (3 T.)
- Sriracha (.25 C.)

Directions:

1. Start by heating your oven to 375 degrees.
2. In a bowl, mix together the salt, pepper, garlic powder, green onion, breadcrumbs, and the turkey. Once this is done, you will want to shape the mix into balls around 1 inch or so. This recipe should make about 40 balls.

3. When the balls are made, place them on a greased baking sheet and pop them in the oven for twenty-five minutes or until they turn a nice, brown color.
4. While these are cooking, you will want to make the sauce. Take a small bowl and combine the ingredients from the list above. Place it in a small pan over a medium heat and allow it to simmer for ten minutes.
5. Finally, toss the balls in the sauce, portion into your containers, and serve with vegetables or even brown rice!

Easy Turkey Chili

Eight Servings

Serving Size: One Cup

Carbohydrates: 26g

Proteins: 35g

Fats: 4g

Ingredients:

- Cayenne Pepper (.10 t.)
- Oregano (2 t.)
- Chili Powder (3 T.)
- Stevia (1 Packet)
- Pepper (.50 t.)
- Salt (.50 t.)
- Jalapenos (2)
- Bell Peppers (2)
- Kidney Beans (1 Can)
- Hot Sauce (.50 t.)
- Tomato Paste (3 T.)
- Diced Tomatoes (1 Can)
- Crushed Tomatoes (1 Can)
- Olive Oil (1 T.)
- Garlic (5)
- Onion (1)
- Ground Turkey (2 Lbs.)

Directions:

1. To start, you will want to place your olive oil, onion, and garlic into a large pot and allow this to cook for a couple of minutes. Once you can smell the garlic, add in your turkey and cook it for ten minutes or until it is brown.

2. Finally, toss in the rest of the ingredients from the list above. Be sure to stir everything together so it becomes well combined. Allow this to cook for an hour over a low heat and then portion into your containers.

Slow Cooker Tomato and Beef Stew
Eight Servings
Serving Size: One and a Half Cups
Carbohydrates: 25g
Proteins: 28g
Fats: 14g
Ingredients:

- Bay Leaf (1)
- Rosemary (2 t.)
- Thyme (1 T.)
- Garlic Powder (2 t.)
- Pepper (.50 t.)
- Salt (1 t.)
- Potatoes (1 lb.)
- Peas (1 C.)
- Celery (3)
- Carrots (3)
- Onion (1)
- Worcestershire Sauce (1 T.)
- Beef Broth (2 C.)
- Tomato Paste (1 Can)
- Stewed Tomatoes (1 Can)
- Stew Beef (2 Lbs.)
- Olive Oil (1 T.)

Directions:

1. This recipe can be made in a number of different ways including instant pot, slow cooker, and even over your stove top.
2. If you are using a slow cooker, pop all of the ingredients from the list above into it and cook on low for about eight hours. As for stovetop, you will want to cook the meat first and then cook in a large pot with the rest of the ingredients for about three hours over a low heat.
3. Either way, allow the meat to cook through, portion into your containers, and enjoy!

Slow Cooked BBQ Pulled Pork
Eight Servings
Serving Size: 1 C.
Carbohydrates: 50g
Proteins: 22g
Fats: 5g
Ingredients:

- Whole Wheat Hamburger Buns (8)
- BBQ Sauce (1 Bottle)
- Diet Root Beer (1 Can)
- Pork Tenderloin (2 Lbs.)

Directions:

1. For a quick dinner, this is the perfect recipe for a delicious dinner.
2. First, pop the tenderloin onto the bottom of the slow cooker. Once in place, pour the diet root beer and BBQ sauce over the top.
3. Cook the tenderloin on low for about seven hours.
4. Once this time is up, shred the tenderloin and serve with your favorite vegetable.

Creamy Slow Cooked Pot Roast
Twelve Servings
Serving Size: 1 C.
Carbohydrates: 5g
Proteins: 46g
Fats: 24g
Ingredients:

- Pot Roast (5.50 Lbs.)
- Water (1.25 C.)
- Dry Onion Soup Mix (1 Packet)
- Cream of Mushroom Soup (2 Cans)

Directions:

1. Begin by placing the mushroom soup, water, and onion soup mix into the bottom of your slow cooker.
2. Gently place the pot roast over the mixture and spoon it over the top. Be sure that it is covered completely before placing the lid on.
3. For a quicker cook, put the roast on high for four hours. For a slower cook, nine hours on low.
4. In the end, turn off the heat, portion out the roast into your containers and serve with a favorite vegetable recipe.

Baked Taco Pie
Eight Servings
Serving Size: 1 Square
Carbohydrates: 37g
Proteins: 20g
Fats: 19g
Ingredients:

- Corn Chips (1 C.)
- Corn (.50 C.)
- Olive Oil (1 T.)
- Honey (1 T.)
- Egg (1)
- Milk (.33 C.)
- Corn Bread Mix (1 Package)
- Black Beans (1 Can)
- Salsa (1 C.)
- Taco Seasoning (1 Packet)
- Ground Beef (1 Lb.)

Directions:

1. Start off by heating your oven to 350 degrees.
2. While this warms up, you will want to take the time to cook the ground beef. Place it in a skillet over medium heat. Once it is browned, toss in the taco seasoning, salsa, and black beans. Cook for several more minutes and then remove from the heat.
3. Next, take a small bowl and mix together the olive oil, honey, egg, milk, and cornbread mix. Once it is in a smooth consistency, pour into the bottom of a casserole dish.

4. Now, layer your ground beef and sprinkle the corn chips over the top.
5. Pop the whole dish into the oven and cook for thirty-five minutes. Once it is cooked through, remove and cut into eight different pieces. Portion and place in containers for an easy lunch or dinner on the go.

Easy Baked Beef Lasagna
Twelve Servings
Serving Size: 1 C.
Carbohydrates: 37g
Proteins: 30g
Fats: 22g
Ingredients:

- Parmesan Cheese (.75 C.)
- Mozzarella Cheese (.75 Lbs.)
- Salt (.50 t.)
- Egg (1)
- Ricotta Cheese (16 Oz.)
- Lasagna Noodles (12)
- Parsley (.25 t.)
- Italian Seasoning (1 t.)
- Fennel Seeds (.50 t.)
- Basil Leaves (1.50 t.)
- Sugar (2 T.)
- Water (.50 C.)
- Tomato Sauce (2 Cans)
- Tomato Paste (2 Cans)
- Crushed Tomatoes (1 Can)
- Garlic (2)
- Onion (.50 C.)
- Ground Beef (.75 Lbs.)

Directions:

1. To begin, take a medium skillet and begin to heat it over a medium heat. Once warm, begin to cook the ground beef until it turns brown.

2. Once the beef is cooked, add in the tomato paste, tomato sauce, and the crushed tomatoes along with the water.
3. When everything is boiling, you can use this time to toss in a tablespoon of salt, pepper, parsley, fennel seeds, basil, and sugar.
4. Put a lid on the skillet and lower the heat. Allow this to cook for about an hour or so in a simmer.
5. While this is simmering, bring a pot of water to a boil over high heat. Once the water is boiling, you can toss in the lasagna noodles and cook for ten minutes or so. Once they are done, drain and set to the side.
6. In another bowl, combine the egg, parsley, salt, and ricotta cheese all together.
7. When these two steps are done, bring your oven to 375 degrees.
8. In a baking dish, begin to arrange your lasagna. You will do this by layering the meat sauce on the bottom of the dish followed by a layer of ricotta cheese, topped by some mozzarella cheese. Continue this until the baking dish is ¾ full.
9. Pop the whole baking dish into the oven once you have covered it with tin foil. Cook everything for twenty-five minutes before removing from the oven.
10. Once cool, portion into containers and enjoy your healthy meal!

Simple Meatloaf Dinner

Eight Servings
Serving Size: 1 C.
Carbohydrates: 19g
Proteins: 19g
Fats: 25g
Ingredients:

- Ketchup (.33 C.)
- Mustard (2 T.)
- Brown Sugar (2 T.)
- Salt (.50 t.)
- Pepper (.50 t.)
- Bread Crumbs (1 C.)
- Milk (1 C.)
- Onion (1)
- Egg (1)
- Ground Beef (1.50 Lbs.)

Directions:

1. Start off by heating your oven to 350 degrees.
2. In a mixing bowl, combine the bread crumbs, milk, egg, onion, and the ground beef. Be sure to combine it well so all of the ingredients are well blended.
3. Place this mixture into a baking dish and set to the side.
4. In another bowl, mix together the mustard, ketchup, and brown sugar. Once this is well blended, gently pour it over the meatloaf.
5. Finally, pop the meatloaf into the oven for about an hour or until the beef is cooked through.
6. Cut the meatloaf into twelve slices and portion out according to your needs.

Chapter Five: Seafood Recipes
Grilled Onion and Peppers Tilapia Tacos

Four Servings
Serving Size: Two Tacos
Carbohydrates: 32g
Proteins: 33g
Fats: 5g
Ingredients:

- Lime (1)
- Jalapeno Pepper (1)
- Corn Tortillas (8)
- Tilapia (4)
- Black Pepper (.50 t.)
- Salt (.50 t.)
- Sweet Bell Peppers (3)
- Onion (2)

Directions:

1. This recipe is recommended to be cooked on the grill for maximum taste but can be done over the stove top as well. To start, you will be cooking the bell peppers and onions over medium heat. This should take ten to fifteen minutes. Season them with salt and pepper to taste.
2. Once the vegetables are cooked through, season your fish and cook in a pan for around three minutes on each side. Once the fish is cooked through, it will become flakey.
3. Finally, assemble the tacos by placing fish, onion mix, and jalapeno slices into the tortillas. If desired, serve with a slice of lime for some extra flavor.

Spicy Crab Stuffed Cucumber Cups

Six Servings
Serving Size: 3 Cups
Carbohydrates: 5g
Proteins: 9g
Fats: 2g
Ingredients:

- Green Onion (1 T.)
- Black Pepper (.50 t.)
- Salt (.50 t.)
- Crab Meat (.75 C.)
- Cream Cheese (.25 C.)
- Sour Cream (.25 C.)
- Cucumbers (3)
- Paprika (Optional)

Directions:

1. Begin by prepping your cucumbers. You can do this by washing, peeling, and cutting them into two-inch slices.
2. If you have a melon baller, scoop out a hole in the center of each cucumber piece. Once this is done, you can set the cucumber aside.
3. In a small bowl, blend the sour cream and cream cheese together. Once they are smooth, add in the rest of the ingredients.
4. Spoon in the crab mixture into the cucumber cups, and they are ready to be served. For some extra flavor, try sprinkling paprika over the tops!

Spicy Cilantro Shrimp
Four Servings
Serving Size: Six Ounces
Carbohydrates: .5g
Proteins: 35g
Fats: 3g
Ingredients:

- Shrimp (2 Lbs.)
- Cinnamon (.10 t.)
- Cayenne Pepper (.10 t.)
- Curry Powder (.10 t.)
- Ground Cumin (.50 t.)
- Paprika (1 t.)
- Salt (.75 t.)
- Cilantro (Pinch)
- Lime (Optional)

Directions:

1. Begin by making the seasoning for your shrimp. Do this by taking a small bowl and combining the cinnamon, cayenne pepper, curry powder, cumin, paprika, and salt.
2. If you are to cook your shrimp on the grill, it is suggested to skewer the shrimp after seasoning them and cooking them for a minute or two over high heat.
3. As for pan frying, bring olive oil to a sizzle over medium heat and cook the shrimp on both sides for five minutes.
4. For some extra flavor, squeeze the juice of a lime over the top and finish with some fresh chopped cilantro. Portion into containers and you will have a delicious dinner waiting for you.

Roasted Shrimp with Lemon Spaghetti Squash
Four Servings
Serving Size: Two Cups of Spaghetti Squash and Five Shrimp
Carbohydrates: 26g
Proteins: 10g
Fats: 11g
Ingredients:

- Parsley (2 T.)
- Greek Yogurt (.25 C.)
- Red Pepper Flakes (.25 t.)
- Dijon Mustard (1 t.)
- White Wine (.50 C.)
- Lemon Zest (1 t.)
- Garlic (3)
- Salt (.50 t.)
- Pepper (.50 t.)
- Butter (2 T.)
- Olive Oil (1 T.)
- Shrimp (12 Oz.)
- Spaghetti Squash (2)

Directions:

1. Begin by heating your oven to 350 degrees.
2. While the oven heats up, begin to prepare your squash by cutting it down the middle, removing the seeds, and popping it onto a lightly greased baking sheet. You will place the squash in the oven for about forty-five minutes.
3. While the squash cooks, you will want to cook your shrimp in a large skillet over medium heat. Season with

salt and pepper to taste and add garlic. This should take four to five minutes to cook the shrimp on either side.
4. Once the shrimp is mostly cooked through, add in the red pepper flakes, Dijon mustard, white wine, lemon zest, and lemon juice, bring this to a boil and then reduce the heat. You will allow this to simmer until the squash is cooked.
5. When the squash is tender, remove from the oven and scrape out the insides.
6. Take the insides, mix together with the sauce and the Greek yogurt. Blend it all together and then scoop back into the squash shell for a delicious meal.

Avocado and Spicy Tuna Wraps

Four Servings
Serving Size: One Wrap
Carbohydrates: 29g
Proteins: 18g
Fats: 2g
Ingredients:

- Whole Wheat Tortillas (4)
- Carrots (1 C.)
- Lettuce (2 C.)
- Salt (.50 t.)
- Pepper (.50 t.)
- Cilantro (1 T.)
- Green Onion (2)
- Onion (2 T.)
- Celery (3 T.)
- Dijon Mustard (1 T.)
- Sriracha (2 T.)
- Avocado (1)
- Tuna (2 Cans)

Directions:

1. In a small bowl, combine the tuna and avocado.
2. Once this is done, you will want to stir in the rest of the ingredients. Use salt and pepper to desired taste.
3. Once this is done, place the mixture into each tortilla wrap and top with the lettuce and carrots. Roll the wraps up tightly, and you have a quick and easy lunch or dinner.

Jerk Caribbean Shrimp
Four Servings
Serving Size: 1 Cup
Carbohydrates: 36g
Proteins: 24g
Fats: 13g
Ingredients:

- Jalapeno (1 T.)
- Green Onion (2 T.)
- Soy Sauce (1 T.)
- Brown Sugar (1 Packet)
- Orange Juice (2 T.)
- Red Wine Vinegar (2 T.)
- Olive Oil (2 T.)
- Shrimp (10 Oz.)

Seasoning:

- Salt (.10 t.)
- Cayenne Pepper (.10 t.)
- Nutmeg (.10 t.)
- Allspice (.10 t.)
- Paprika (.50 t.)
- Thyme (.25 t.)
- Onion Powder (.25 t.)
- Garlic Powder (.50 t.)

Directions:

1. You will begin by making the marinade for the shrimp. You will do this by taking a small bowl and mixing together the following: seasonings, orange juice, red wine vinegar, soy sauce, green onion, brown sugar, jalapeno, and the olive oil. Once this is well blended, add in your shrimp and allow this to soak for about thirty minutes.
2. Place the shrimp on skewers and cook over a medium heat for five or six minutes on either side.
3. Serve the shrimp with your favorite rice or vegetable for a complete and healthy meal.

One Sheet Soy and Ginger Glazed Salmon

Four Servings

Serving Size: One Fillet of Salmon with Half Cup of Carrots and Fourth Cup of Green Beans

Carbohydrates: 25g

Proteins: 48g

Fats: 12g

Ingredients:

- Salt (.50 t.)
- Pepper (.50 t.)
- Olive Oil (1 T.)
- Carrots (2 C.)
- Green Beans (1 Lb.)
- Salmon Fillets (4)

Sauce:

- Green Onions (1 T.)
- Garlic (2)
- Ginger (1 T.)
- Honey (1 T.)
- Sweet Chili Sauce (2 T.)
- Soy Sauce (.25 C.)

Directions:

1. Before you begin cooking, bring your oven to 400 degrees.
2. On a baking sheet, place your green beans, carrots, and salmon skin side down. Drizzle all of the above ingredients with the olive oil and salt and pepper to taste.

3. Take a small bowl and mix together the green onion, garlic, ginger, honey, chili sauce, and the soy sauce. Once this is smooth, spoon it over the salmon and pop the whole pan into the oven.
4. Cook the pan for ten minutes and then turn on the broiler for three minutes so that the salmon comes out crisp.
5. Portion out your meal and dinner will be all ready for you!

Crusted Hummus Salmon

Four Servings
Serving Size: One Salmon Fillet
Carbohydrates: 14g
Proteins: 48g
Fats: 27g
Ingredients:

- Honey (2 t.)
- Dijon Mustard (1.50 t.)
- Butter (.25 C.)
- Thyme (2 t.)
- Parmesan Cheese (.25 C.)
- Panko Breadcrumbs (.50 C.)
- Hummus (.25 C.)
- Salmon Fillets (4)
- Salt (.50 t.)
- Pepper (.50 t.)

Directions:

1. To begin, heat your oven to 375 degrees.
2. Place the salmon fillets onto a baking sheet and season them with salt and pepper to taste. Once this is done, you can spoon a thin layer of hummus over the top of them.
3. In a small bowl, mix together the butter, honey, Dijon mustard, panko bread crumbs, thyme, and parmesan cheese. Once this is well combined, you can go ahead and press it onto each salmon fillet.
4. Bake these for twenty minutes or until the fish becomes flaky. Portion and go!

Crab Cake Baked Balls
Eight Servings
Serving Size: Three Balls
Carbohydrates: 12g
Proteins: 13g
Fats: 1g
Ingredients:

- Black Pepper (.10 t.)
- Salt (.10 t.)
- Panko Breadcrumbs (1 C.)
- Crab Meat (1 Lb.)
- Old Bay Seasoning (1.50 t.)
- Green Onions (2)
- Lemon Juice (2 t.)
- Sriracha (.25 t.)
- Dijon Mustard (1 T.)
- Greek Yogurt (.25 C.)
- Egg (1)

Directions:

1. Start by heating your oven to 350 degrees.
2. While this warms up, take a bowl and mix together the old bay seasoning, lemon juice, green onion, egg, yogurt, and Sriracha. Once this is well combined, you can also add in the crab meat.
3. With this mixture, form one inch balls and place them on a greased sheet. You should be able to make about twenty-four balls with this mixture. Once this is done, pop them into the fridge for thirty minutes.

4. Finally, pop the balls into the oven for thirty minutes. When they are done, they should be a nice golden color. For even crispier balls, try putting them in the broiler for another five minutes.
5. Portion into your containers and this makes an excellent snack or salad topper.

Spicy Moroccan Salmon

Four Servings
Serving Size: One Salmon Fillet
Carbohydrates: 32g
Proteins: 50g
Fats: 14g
Ingredients:

- Salt (.50 t.)
- Pepper (.50 t.)
- Cilantro (1 T.)

- Salmon Fillets (4)

Sauce:

- Smoked Paprika (1 t.)
- Garlic (3)
- Honey (1 T.)
- Ginger (1.50 t.)
- Lemon Juice (1 T.)
- Olive Oil (1 T.)
- Harissa (3 T.)

Directions:

1. Start off by heating your oven to 400 degrees.
2. Take heavy duty tin foil and lay them out onto a baking sheet.
3. Carefully season the salmon with the salt and pepper and place them skin side down into the tin foil.
4. In a small bowl, mix together all of the sauce ingredients from the list above. Be sure that they are well blended and then spoon them over the fillets of salmon.
5. Fold the tin foil over the fish and bake in the oven for twenty minutes. This should be enough time to cook the salmon through so it is nice and flakey.
6. For some extra flavor, add some chopped cilantro when you portion into your containers.

Chapter Six: Vegetable Recipes
Garlic Roasted Cauliflower

Six Servings
Serving Size: .50 C.
Carbohydrates: 9g
Proteins: 5g
Fats: 9g
Ingredients:

- Parsley (1 T.)
- Salt (.50 t.)
- Pepper (.50 t.)
- Parmesan Cheese (.33 C.)
- Cauliflower (1)
- Olive Oil (3 T.)
- Garlic (2 T.)

Directions:

1. Start out by heating your oven to 450 degrees.
2. While this warms up, take a large baking dish and place your cauliflower. Sprinkle the garlic and olive oil over the top.
3. Finally, season with salt and pepper to taste.
4. Pop the dish into the oven and cook for a total of twenty-five minutes. Halfway through, remove the dish and sprinkle the parmesan cheese on and then broil for five minutes. This will turn the cauliflower a nice golden brown color.
5. Portion out the cauliflower and serve with a favorite protein.

Parmesan Asparagus
Five Servings
Serving Size: .50 C.
Carbohydrates: 5g
Proteins: 8g
Fats:18g
Ingredients:

- Salt (.50 t.)
- Pepper (.50 t.)
- Parmesan Cheese (.75 C.)
- Asparagus (1 Lb.)
- Olive Oil (.25 C.)
- Butter (1 T.)

Directions:

1. Begin by heating a medium skillet over medium heat. Place your tablespoon of butter and olive oil and bring to a sizzle.
2. Once the olive oil and butter are heated, toss in the asparagus and stir for ten minutes.
3. When the asparagus is cooked through, remove any extra oil, sprinkle on the parmesan cheese and salt and pepper to taste.
4. Portion out the asparagus and enjoy with any lunch or dinner for delicious meal prep.

Parsley and Lemon Green Beans

Four Servings

Serving Size: .50 C.

Carbohydrates: 13g

Proteins: 3g

Fats: 9g

Ingredients:

- Lemon (1)
- Salt (.50 t.)
- Pepper (.50 t.)
- Parsley (.25 C.)
- Lemon Zest (1 T.)
- Garlic (3)
- Olive Oil (2 t.)
- Butter (2 T.)
- Green Beans (1 Lb.)
- White Sugar (.10 t.)

Directions:

1. Begin by bringing a pot of water to a boil. Once the water is boiling, toss in a pinch of white sugar and your green beans. Allow these to cook for five minutes or until they are tender.
2. In a large skillet, heat up the olive oil over medium heat. Add in the butter next and allow it to melt before tossing in the garlic and green beans.
3. Season the beans with the parsley, pepper, salt, and lemon zest. Cook this combination for another couple of minutes.
4. Finally, portion out your side dish and enjoy.

Fried Green Tomatoes
Four Servings
Serving Size: .25 C.
Carbohydrates: 57g
Proteins: 13g
Fats: 27g
Ingredients:

- Vegetable Oil (1 Q.)
- Black Pepper (.50 t.)
- Salt (.50 t.)
- Bread Crumbs (.50 C.)
- Cornmeal (.50 C.)
- All-purpose Flour (1 C.)
- Milk (.50 C.)
- Eggs (2)
- Green Tomatoes (4)

Directions:

1. To start, pour the vegetable oil into a large pan and begin to heat it up into a medium heat.
2. While the oil heats, you will want to prepare your tomatoes by slicing them into .50 inch thick pieces. Be sure to throw the ends out as you will have no need for them.
3. In a bowl, mix together the milk and the eggs.
4. Place your flour onto a plate and line up with the bowl that is holding the milk and eggs.
5. On a third plate, mix together your breadcrumbs, cornmeal, pepper, and salt.

6. Now that these are prepared, dip your tomato pieces in the liquid mixture, the flour, and then the breadcrumb mixture. Be sure to coat the tomatoes before tossing them into the vegetable oil.
7. Fry the tomatoes for five minutes on either side or until golden brown.
8. Portion them out and enjoy as a side dish or a nice, healthy snack!

Grilled Herbed Artichokes
Four Servings
Serving Size: .50 C.
Carbohydrates: 19g
Proteins: 6g
Fats: 14g
Ingredients:

- Butter (.25 C.)
- Artichokes (4)
- Lemon (1)
- Salt (1 t.)
- White Wine (.25 C.)
- Olive Oil (1 t.)
- Liquid Smoke Flavor (.50 t.)
- Thyme (.25 t.)
- Basil (.25 t.)
- Italian Seasoning (.50 t.)

Directions:

1. Begin by placing a pot filled with water over medium heat. As the water begins to boil, add in the liquid smoke, white wine, salt, olive oil, basil, thyme, and Italian seasoning.
2. Once this is done, squeeze in the lemon juice and drop the whole thing into the pot.
3. When the water is boiling, toss in the artichoke and cook for thirty minutes.
4. Remove the artichoke from the water, remove any excess water and portion out.

Sweet Glazed Carrots

Eight Servings

Serving Size: 1 C.

Carbohydrates: 18g

Proteins: 2g

Fats: 6g

Ingredients:

- Pepper (.25 t.)
- Salt (.25 t.)
- Brown Sugar (.25 C.)
- Butter (.25 C.)
- Carrots (2 Lbs.)

Directions:

1. To start, pour water into a large saucepan and bring it to a boil. Once the water is boiling, add in the carrots and reduce the heat to simmer the carrots for ten minutes. When the carrots are nice and soft, drain the water and place them into a bowl to the side.
2. In the same saucepan, begin to melt the butter. Once it is melted, add in the pepper, salt, and brown sugar. Gently toss the carrots into the sauce and cook them for five more minutes or so.
3. Finally, turn off the heat and allow the carrots to cool. Place a cup to each container, and you have a great snack or side dish for any lunch or dinner.

Lemon and Garlic Roasted Broccoli

Six Servings

Serving Size: .50 C.

Carbohydrates: 7g

Proteins: 3g

Fats: 2g

Ingredients:

- Lemon Juice (.50 t.)
- Garlic (1)
- Black Pepper (.50 t.)
- Salt (1 t.)
- Olive Oil (2 t.)
- Broccoli (2)

Directions:

1. Begin heating your oven to 400 degrees.
2. In a bowl, mix the pepper, salt, garlic, olive oil, and broccoli all together. Be sure that the broccoli is evenly coated to assure the best flavor.
3. Place the broccoli onto a baking sheet and cook for twenty minutes or until the vegetable becomes soft and tender.
4. Finally, squeeze lemon liberally over the broccoli, portion, and enjoy.

Simple Roasted Asparagus
Four Servings
Serving Size: .50 C.
Carbohydrates: 6g
Proteins: 4g
Fats: 11g
Ingredients:

- Lemon Juice (1 T.)
- Black Pepper (.50 t.)
- Salt (1 T.)
- Garlic (1)
- Olive Oil (3 T.)
- Asparagus (1 Bunch)

Directions:

1. You can start out by heating your oven to 425 degrees.
2. While this warms up, place your asparagus in a bowl and coat it with olive oil. Once it is well covered, toss in the salt, pepper, and lemon juice and be sure to season it well.
3. Finally, place the asparagus onto a baking sheet and pop into the oven for fifteen minutes.
4. Remove from the oven, portion out into your containers, and enjoy your healthy side.

Roasted Butternut Squash
Four Servings
Serving Size: 1 C.
Carbohydrates: 31g
Proteins: 3g
Fats: 7g
Ingredients:

- Salt (.50 t.)
- Pepper (.50 t.)
- Garlic (2)
- Olive Oil (2 T.)
- Butternut Squash (1)

Directions:

1. Start off this recipe by heating your oven to 400 degrees.
2. Next, prepare your butternut squash by cutting it into cubes and tossing in olive oil and garlic. You can also season with salt and pepper if you desire.
3. Finally, arrange the squash onto a baking sheet and cook for thirty minutes or so.
4. Remove the squash from the oven, cool, and portion out into your containers.

Cilantro and Lime Cauliflower Rice

Four Servings

Serving Size: .50 C.

Carbohydrates: 10g

Proteins: 4g

Fats: 6g

Ingredients:

- Butter (2 T.)
- Cilantro (.50 C.)
- Lime (1)
- Water (1 T.)
- Cauliflower (1)

Directions:

1. To start off, you will want to grate the cauliflower. If you have a food processor, stick it in there and pulse until the cauliflower begins to resemble rice.
2. Once it is created, place it in the microwave for seven minutes or so. This should be enough time to make the cauliflower become soft and tender.
3. Finally, remove the rice from the microwave. When it has cooled, toss in the lime juice, lime zest, butter, and cilantro. Mix everything together well and then portion into your containers. This is an excellent carb replacement if you are trying to lose weight.

Chapter Seven: Dessert Recipes
Avocado Chocolate Pudding

Six Servings
Serving Size: .50 C.
Carbohydrates: 21g
Proteins: 3g
Fats: 10g

Ingredients:

- Salt (.50 t.)
- Vanilla Extract (2 t.)
- Vanilla Almond Milk (.50 C.)
- Greek Yogurt (2 T.)
- Honey (.25 C.)
- Unsweetened Cocoa Powder (.50 C.)
- Avocados (2)

Directions:

1. Simply take all of the ingredients from above and place it into a blender. Pulse the ingredients until they become a creamy, smooth consistency.
2. For some extra flavor, top with your favorite whipped cream. Portion and you have a quick, healthy dessert!

Lemon and Blueberry Bread Pudding

Four Servings

Serving Size: 1 C.

Carbohydrates: 44g

Proteins: 9g

Fats: 5g

Ingredients:

- Blueberries (1 Pint)
- Lemon (1)
- Salt (.25 t.)
- Vanilla Extract (.50 t.)
- Brown Sugar (1 T.)
- Honey (1 T.)
- Eggs (2)
- Unsweetened Applesauce (.50 C.)
- Almond Milk (1.50 C.)
- Whole Wheat Bread (5 C.)

Directions:

1. Begin by heating your oven to 350 degrees.
2. While this warms up, take a small bowl to combine the lemon zest, salt, vanilla extract, brown sugar, honey, eggs, applesauce, and milk. Gently whisk everything together until it is well combined.
3. Next, chop up the bread into two inch cubes. Once this is done, fold the bread and blueberries into the egg mixture.
4. Place all of these ingredients into a bowl and allow to soak in the fridge for an hour or so.
5. Pop the baking dish into the oven for fifty minutes to an hour and cook until it comes out a golden brown color.

6. Portion out the dessert and microwave when you want a healthy dessert.

Pumpkin Spice Mug Cake

One Serving
Serving Size: One Mug Cake
Carbohydrates: 35g
Proteins: 5g
Fats: 1g
Ingredients:

- Vanilla Extract (.25 t.)
- Unsweetened Apple Sauce (1.50 t.)
- Almond Milk (2 T.)
- Pumpkin Puree (2 t.)
- Maple Syrup (1 T.)
- Nutmeg (.10 t.)
- Pumpkin Pie Spice (.25 t.)
- Cinnamon (.25 t.)
- Baking Powder (.50 t.)
- Whole Wheat Flour (4 T.)

Directions:

1. In your favorite mug, first, you will want to mix together all of the dry ingredients from the list above.
2. Once this is done, one by one stir in your wet ingredients. Stir everything together to assure there are no clumps in your cake.
3. Pop the mug into the microwave for one minute.
4. Allow the cake to cool before you enjoy!

Sweet Apple Oatmeal Cider Crisp

Eight Servings

Serving Size: .75 C.

Carbohydrates: 43g

Proteins: 4g

Fats: 10g

Ingredients:

- Cinnamon Sticks (2)
- Maple Syrup (.33 C.)
- Apple Cider (2 C.)
- Apples (6)

Topping:

- Salt (.25 t.)
- Allspice (.25 t.)
- Cinnamon (1 t.)
- Vanilla Extract (1 t.)
- Apple Cider Mix (.25 C.)
- Almond Flour (.50 C and 2 T.)
- Pecans (.50 C.)
- Rolled Oats (1 C.)

Directions:

1. Begin by heating your oven to 375 degrees.
2. While this heats up, begin to prepare your apples by peeling them and slicing them. Once this is done, toss them in a large bowl and set it to the side.
3. Next, take a saucepan and heat it over a high heat. Once it is warm, add in your cinnamon sticks, maple syrup, and apple cider and bring to a boil. When it begins to boil, turn

down the heat and simmer this mix for twenty minutes or so.
4. After the time has passed, remove the sticks and pour the warm mixture over the apples. You will want to save .25 C. of this liquid for later use.
5. Once this step has been done, take another bowl and combine the following: salt, allspice, cinnamon, vanilla, apple cider mix, almond flour, pecans, and rolled oats. Be sure to combine everything together well.
6. Next, toss the soaked apples into a baking dish and cover with the crumbled top.
7. Now, it is time to place the baking dish into the oven for thirty minutes.
8. In the end, the recipe will be golden brown. Remove from the oven, allow to cool, and then portion for a healthy dessert option.

Peanut Butter and Apple Cookies
Eighteen Servings
Serving Size: One Cookie
Carbohydrates: 10g
Proteins: 3g
Fats: 6g
Ingredients:

- White Chocolate Chips (.25 C.)
- Apple Pie Spice (.25 t.)
- Ground Flax Seed (2 T.)
- Peanuts (2 T.)
- Dried Apples (.33 C.)
- Rolled Oats (1 C.)
- Rice Cereal (1 C.)
- Vanilla Extract (.50 t.)
- Honey (2 T.)
- Peanut Butter (.33 C.)
- Coconut Oil (4 T.)

Directions:

1. To start out, begin to melt the vanilla, honey, peanut butter, and coconut oil in a saucepan over low heat. Continue to melt this mixture until the ingredients are well blended and smooth.
2. Remove the pan from the heat and stir in all other ingredients minus the white chocolate chips.
3. Now, take the mixture and create small balls. Place these onto a baking sheet and pop them into the fridge for twenty minutes.

4. For some extra flavor, melt the white chocolate chips and drizzle over the top.
5. Portion out the cookies and save for a sweet treat.

Simple Chocolate Chip Cookies
Fifteen Servings
Serving Size: Two Cookies
Carbohydrates: 17g
Proteins: 4g
Fats: 10g
Ingredients:

- Dark Chocolate Chips (.50 C.)
- Vanilla Extract (1 t.)
- Honey (.25 C.)
- Coconut Oil (5 T.)
- Eggs (2)
- Salt (.25 t.)
- Baking Soda (1 t.)
- Almond Flour (.50 C.)
- Whole Wheat Flour (1.50 C.)

Directions:

1. Start off by heating your oven to 350 degrees.
2. While this warms up, line a cookie sheet with parchment paper, so it is ready.
3. Now, take a small bowl and mix together the baking soda, almond flour, whole wheat flour, and set it to the side.
4. In a mixer, blend together the vanilla, honey, coconut oil, and eggs. As this blends, slowly add in the flour mixture until everything is well combined.
5. When you are ready, fold in the dark chocolate chips and carefully spoon a tablespoon of this mixture onto the cooking sheet. There should be about thirty balls at the end.

6. Pop the cookie sheet into the oven for ten minutes or until they are a nice golden color.
7. Remove the cookies from the oven, cool, and portion out!

Quinoa and Peanut Butter No Bake Balls

Twelve Servings
Serving Size: One Ball
Carbohydrates: 17g
Proteins: 5g
Fats: 6g
Ingredients:

- Salt (.10 t.)
- Cinnamon (.50 t.)
- Vanilla Extract (1 t.)
- Maple Syrup (.25 C.)
- Peanut Butter (.33 C.)
- Sunflower Seeds (.25 C.)
- Raisins (.33 C.)
- Coconut, Shredded (3 T.)
- Rolled Oats (1 C.)
- Cooked Quinoa (1 C.)

Directions:

1. Start off by mixing all of the ingredients together in a bowl. If you have a blender, this will make it even easier.
2. Once the dough is formed, roll the mix into balls and place them on a pan.
3. Pop the pan into the fridge and allow the balls to cool for a couple of hours.
4. These balls are great for a quick snack during the day or a sweet treat when you need one.

Thin Funfetti Cookies

Thirty Servings
Serving Size: One Cookie
Carbohydrates: 15g
Proteins: 1g
Fats: 2g
Ingredients:

- Eggs (2)
- Vanilla Yogurt (.50 C.)
- Funfetti Cake Mix (1 Box)

Directions:

1. Start off by heating your oven to 375 degrees.
2. While this warms up, mix together the cake mix with the eggs and the fat-free yogurt. Mix everything together until there are no longer clumps.
3. Next, take out a cookie sheet and cover with tin foil. Carefully spoon out the mix onto the cookie sheet and pop into the oven for twelve minutes or so.
4. Remove cookies when they turn brown on the bottoms, portion, and enjoy a small treat.

Skinny Watermelon Icey Pops

Twelve Servings
Serving Size: One Pop
Carbohydrates: 17g
Proteins: 1g
Fats: 2g
Ingredients:

- Lime Sherbet (1 Pint)
- Mini Chocolate Chips (.25 C.)
- Sugar (.50 C.)
- Watermelon Pulp-Seeded (5 C.)

Directions:

1. Begin by placing the watermelon and sugar into a blender and pulsing until it becomes smooth. Next, strain this mixture into a bowl and pop into the freezer until the mix becomes slushy. This should take around three hours.
2. Once you have a slush, fold in the chocolate chips and pour into disposable cups. When this step is done, place the cups into your freezer for two hours or so. After two hours, the cups should be solid but not frozen.
3. Now, spread the lime sherbet over the top and insert the Popsicle sticks.
4. For best results, leave the pops in overnight to allow them to freeze completely.

Raspberry and Chocolate Grain-Free Mini Cakes

Twelve Servings
Serving Size: One Cake
Carbohydrates: 18g
Proteins: 6g
Fats: 15g
Ingredients:

- Raspberry Preserves (4 T.)
- Maple Syrup (.50 C.)
- Coconut Oil (.25 C.)
- Almond Milk (.50 C.)
- Eggs (3)
- Salt (.25 t.)
- Baking Powder (1.50 t.)
- Cocoa Powder (.75 C.)
- Coconut Flour (2 T.)

- Almond Flour (1.75 C.)
- Fresh Raspberries (1 C.)

Directions:

1. Start off by heating your oven to 350 degrees.
2. While this warms, mix together the coconut flour, almond flour, salt, baking powder, and cocoa powder.
3. In a different bowl, combine the wet ingredients including maple syrup, coconut oil (melted), almond milk, and eggs.
4. Now, combine everything together and fold in the raspberry preserves. Be sure everything is well mixed so that there are no clumps in the mixture.
5. Divide your chocolate batter into greased muffin tins and pop into the heated oven for twenty-five minutes or until baked through.
6. Remove from the oven, cool, and portion for a tasty treat.

Thin Strawberry Cheesecake

Eight Servings
Serving Size: One Slice
Carbohydrates: 29g
Proteins: 4g
Fats: 9g
Ingredients:

- Fresh Strawberries (14)
- Vanilla Extract (2 T.)
- Stevia (6 Packets)
- Reduced-fat Graham Cracker Crust (1)
- Fat-free Cream Cheese (1 Package)
- Cool Whip (8 oz.)

Directions:

1. Start off this recipe by taking a large bowl and mixing together your stevia, vanilla extract, and the cream cheese. You will want to mix these all together until it becomes fluffy. If you want, try to add in some whipped cream to make it even smoother.
2. Next, you will want to spoon this mixture into your pie crust. We suggest using a graham cracker crust, but you can use whatever you like best.
3. Once in place, toss the pie into the fridge for a few hours or until it becomes firm.
4. While the pie firms in the fridge, prep your strawberries by cutting the tops off and cutting them long ways into halves.
5. Finally, remove the pie from the fridge and gently place the strawberry pieces.

6. Slice up the pie, and you have a healthy and delicious dessert for when you need it!

Conclusion

I hope at this point in the book, you are feeling a bit more confident about meal prepping. Remember that this isn't something you have to DIVE into. It is perfectly okay to plan on one meal for the week. This one meal is better than no meals at all. Slowly, you will become surer of your skills and be able to advance to prepping multiple meals in a week. Whether you are doing this for yourself, or your whole family, remember all of the incredible benefits that come with meal prepping!

If you ever feel lost, be sure to refer back to the very first chapter of this book. It will cover all of the basics including tips and tricks, pros and cons, and the basic schedule to follow. If you take anything away, remember to choose a day and take the time. It may seem like you are spending a lot of time cooking but remember that you will be saving that cooking and prepping time through your whole week. Now, you can focus on what you will spend all of this extra time doing! Perhaps it will be taking that exercise class you've been thinking about or some quality family time. Either way, meal prepping can shed new light on a healthier lifestyle.

Hopefully, you have found at least one recipe within these chapters you are excited to try. I tried my very best to include a wide variety of meals for you to prep. Whether you are vegan, vegetarian, or eat everything, there is a recipe out there for you. As I said before, try to start simple. Perhaps grab a breakfast recipe like the overnight oats blueberry muffin style or a simple detox ginger and peach smoothie. The best part is that it is up to you! There is so much flexibility with meal prep, all it takes is a little time and dedication.

If you enjoyed what you learned in this book, it would be appreciated if you would leave a five-star review. The goal is to help as many people out there as possible. I understand that meal prepping can be overwhelming, which is why I have created this book in the first place. Now, I wish you the best of luck on your health journey and remember to enjoy it along the way.

www.ingramcontent.com/pod-product-compliance
Lightning Source LLC
Chambersburg PA
CBHW071341080526
44587CB00017B/2922